The Street of Crocodiles

based on stories by
Bruno Schulz

from an adaptation by
Simon McBurney and Mark Wheatley

devised by
the Company

Methuen Drama

Published by Methuen 1999

5 7 9 10 8 6 4

First published in the United Kingdom in 1999 by
Methuen Publishing Limited
215 Vauxhall Bridge Road, London, SW1V 1EJ

Peribo Pty Ltd, 58 Beaumont Road, Mount Kuring-Gai
NSW 2080, Australia, ACN 002 273 761
(for Australia and New Zealand)

Methuen Publishing Limited Reg. No. 3543167

A CIP catalogue record for this book is available from the British Library

ISBN 0 413 73870 1

Typeset by SX Composing DTP, Rayleigh, Essex

Printed and bound in Great Britain
by Cox & Wyman Ltd, Reading, Berkshire

The Street of Crocodiles
A Republic of Dreams

Based on stories by Bruno Schulz
Adapted by Simon McBurney and Mark Wheatley

This version opened at the Queen's Theatre on 19 January 1999
with the following cast:

Joseph	Cesar Sarachu
The Father	Matthew Scurfield
The Mother	Annabel Arden

The Family
Uncle Charles	Clive Mendus
Agatha	Charlotte Medcalf
Cousin Emil	Antonio Gil Martinez

The Maids
Adela	Bronagh Gallagher
Maria	Ásta Sighvats

The Shop Assistants
Theodore	Eric Mallett
Leon	Stefan Metz

Directed by	Simon McBurney
Design	Rae Smith
Lighting	Paule Constable
Sound	Christopher Shutt

Lighting re-created by	Paul Anderson
Company Stage Manager	Anita Ashwick
Costume Supervisor	Christina Cunningham
Sound Operator	Gareth Fry
Production Management	Gemma Swallow, Ed Wilson

Press and Marketing	Guy Chapman Associates
	0171 379 7474
Production photographer	Joan Marcus

The production runs 1 hour 45 minutes. There is no interval

These performances are dedicated to Jacob Schulz who died in
1997.

Paul Anderson
(Lighting re-creation)

For Complicite: lighting design for *The Chairs* for which he received nominations for an Olivier Award, Drama Desk Award and Tony Award. Production Electrician for the original production of *The Street of Crocodiles*. Relights for *The Three Lives of Lucie Cabrol* and *The Caucasian Chalk Circle*. Recent design includes *Arabian Nights* (Young Vic) and *Cinderella* (Theatre Royal Stratford East)Other work: various designs for the Joseph Rowntree Theatre from 1982 to 1987, *As I Lay Dying*, *Twelfth Night*, *West Side Story* and *Guys and Dolls* (allYoung Vic), *Special Occasions*, *Hospitality* and *Blue Window* for North America Theatre UK, *The Real World* (Soho Poly), *The Double Bass* (Man in the Moon), *Rediscovering Pompie* (IBM exhibition). Production Electrician for *The Last Yankee* (Duke of York's), *A Streetcar Named Desire* (Haymarket / Bill Kenwright) and Hussain Chaylain fashion show (London Fashion Week / Blondstein International).

Annabel Arden
(Performer)

Trained with Philippe Gaulier and Monika Pagneux. Co-founder of Theatre de Complicite. For Complicite: acted in *Foodstuff, Put It On Your Head, Anything For A Quiet Life, The Phantom Violin* and the original production of *The Street of Crocodiles*. Annabel also acted in the TV films *Burning Ambition* and *Anything For A Quiet Life*. Directed: *A Minute Too Late, Please Please Please, The Lamentations of Thel, The Visit* (Best Director, Time Out Awards) and *The Winter's Tale*. Associate collaborator on *The Three Lives of Lucie Cabrol* and *Out of a house walked a man...* Other theatre: Acted in *Playing With Fire* and *Abel Barebone* (Traverse), *No Son of Mine* (Philippe Gaulier's Bouffon play), *1001 Nights* (L'Atelier International de L'Acteur), *Uncle Vanya* (Renaissance Theatre Company). Directed: *India Song* (Theatr Clwyd), *The Women of Troy* (RNT) both co-directed with Annie Castledine. She also co-directed *Out of Here* (a CandoCo dance project). Opera: *Miss Donnithorne's Maggot* by Sir Peter Maxwell Davies (Guildhall), *The Magic Flute* (Opera North), *The Return of Ulysses* (Buxton Festival - Opera North), *Leonore* (conducted by John Eliot Gardiner), *Faust* (Stadtteater, Luzern). Future directing work: *The Dwarf* and *La Traviata* (both for Opera North).Television: *The Mushroom Picker*.

Anita Ashwick
(Company Stage Manager)

Anita was resident Company Stage Manager at the Young Vic Theatre from 1996-98. She has worked with the Thorndike Repertory Theatre, the Theatre of Comedy Company, Triumph Apollo, Bill Kenwright,

Pola Jones and English National Opera. She was CSM for Opera Factory London for three years. For Complicite: *The Three Lives of Lucie Cabrol*, *The Caucasian Chalk Circle* and the original production of *The Street of Crocodiles*.

Paule Constable
(Lighting)

For Complicite: five productions including *The Caucasian Chalk Circle*, T*he Three Lives of Lucie Cabrol* and the original production of *The Street of Crocodiles* (1993 Olivier Award Nomination). Other theatre includes: *More Grimm Tales*, *Twelfth Night*, *As I Lay Dying* (Young Vic), *Uncle Vanya*, Beckett plays, *The Mysteries* (RSC), *Henry IV Parts 1 & 2* (English Touring Theatre) and *The Weir* (Royal Court Theatre). Opera includes: productions for New Zealand International Festival, English National Opera, Opera North and Welsh and Scottish Operas. Ballet: *Bright Young Things* for Birmingham Royal Ballet 1997 seen at the Royal Opera House. Paule is currently designing for the RNT, Young Vic and Manchester Royal Exchange.

Christina Cunningham
(Costume Supervisor)

Trained at Wimbledon School of Art. For Complicite: *The Street of Crocodiles* in Tokyo. Costume Design includes: *De Frofundis, Just Not Fair* (RNT/Birmingham Rep.), *Fire Raisers* (Riverside Studios).

Costume Supervisor for: *The Misanthrope, Hurly Burly, Prayers of Sherkin (*or Peter Hall Company, *Personals, The Boyfriend* segment of *Hey Mr Producer* and Moving Theatre Company's season at Riverside Studios.

Gareth Fry
(Sound Operator)

Originally trained as a recording engineer then in theatre sound design. Recent shows as sound operator include: *Oh What a Lovely War* (RNT national tour and Camden Roundhouse) and *The Lion, the Witch and the Wardrobe (RSC Stratford)*. Designs for theatre include: *Showstoppers* (Arts Theatre), *Clocks and Whistles* (Bush) and *Something About Us* (Lyric Studio). Gareth is a founder member of FP Sound - a collective of sound designers, engineers and composers specialising in artistic sound design for theatre.

Bronagh Gallagher
(Performer)

For Complicite: *The Caucasian Chalk Circle*. Other theatre: *A Patriot Game, A Crucial Week in the Life of a Grocer's Assistant* and *The Iceman Cometh* (Abbey, Dublin), *The Rocky Horror Show* (SFX Centre, Dublin), *Peer Gynt* (Ninagawa Company and Thelma Holt tour), *Portia Coughlan* (Abbey, Dublin and Royal Court). Television: *Dear Sarah, Island of Strangers, Flash McVeigh, Over the Rainbow, Ruffian Hearts, The Shadow of a*

Gunman. Film: *Star Wars, Divorcing Jack, Painted Angels, The Commitments, Mary Reilly, Pulp Fiction* and *This Year's Love.*

Simon McBurney
(Director)

Studied at Cambridge and trained in Paris. Co-founder and Artistic Director of Theatre de Complicite. Since 1983 he has devised, directed and acted in 23 productions with the Company, including *The Street of Crocodiles, The Three Lives of Lucie Cabrol, Out of a house walked a man..., The Caucasian Chalk Circle* and *The Chairs.* Winner of numerous international awards as both actor and director, Simon has also performed extensively in radio and television. Films include: *Kafka, Tom and Viv, Being Human, Mesmer, The Ogre, Cousin Bette* and most recently *Eugene Onegin* with Ralph Fiennes, due for 1999 release.

Antonio Gil Martinez
(Performer)

Born in Spain. Trained at the Conservatorio de Arte Dramatico de Sevilla and L'Ecole Jacques Lecoq, Paris. For Complicite: *The Caucasian Chalk Circle,* and the original production of *The Street of Crocodiles.* Other theatre: Van Gogh in *Diamonds In The Soil* (Dublin Festival), *In Five Years Time* (Southwark Playhouse), *Blood Wedding* (National Theatre of Switzerland) *Waiting for Godot* (Teatro de la Jacara, Seville),

Obsession (co-written with Parti-Pris Theatre Co.), *A Beautiful Life* (Talking Pictures), *Kabaret Bouffons* (NADA Théâtre, Main award 1991 Avignon Festival), *Croquis Marrants* (Théâtre de la Jacquerie, Paris), *Femmes, Guerre, Comédie* (Théâtre Alibi, Corsica), Television: *Laurie Lee, Soldier Soldier* (Carlton), *Sans Frontières* (French TV), *Al Filo de La Ley* (Spanish TV). Film: *The Man with Rain in his Shoes* (released in autumn 1998).

Eric Mallett
(Performer)

Trained at Southampton University and L'Ecole Jacques Lecoq, Paris. For Complicite: *The Visit, The Phantom Violin, The Lamentations of Thel* and the original production of *The Street of Crocodiles.* Other theatre: Dromio of Ephesus in *The Comedy of Errors* (RSC), *The Jungle Book* (Young Vic), *The Taming of the Shrew* (Crucible Theatre), Mike Alfred's production of *The Miser* (Oxford Stage Company), *Gebb* (Rainmaker Picture Story), *We've Been Had* (Faceback Theatre Co.) and *Alice in Wonderland* (Theatre de la Foule). Eric was also Director of Movement for the RSC's production of *Spring Awakening.* Television: *Angels, A Touch of Frost, Peter and The Wolf* (BBC), *Anything For A Quiet Life.* Film: *Paulette* directed by Claude Confortes.

Charlotte Medcalf
(Performer)

For Complicite: *Out of a house walked a man...* Other theatre: *Gormenghast* (David Glass Ensemble), *Porter's Daughter* (Peta Lily and NTC), *Cabaret* (Donmar Warehouse) *Sara, Lady Betty* (Cheek by Jowl) *Romeo and Juliet, Dracula, Measure for Measure, Good Person of Sechzuan* (London Bubble), *Wind in the Willows* (RNT), *The Party Card* (New End Theatre), *Stepping Out* (Hornchurch), *Cyrano* (Greenwich), *The Beaux Stratagem, Low Level Panic* (Liverpool Playhouse Studio), *Fears & Miseries* (Young Vic). Most recently Charlotte appeared as Wendolene in *A Grand Night Out*. Television: *Cabaret, The Bill* and *Playbus*.

Clive Mendus
(Performer)

Trained at L'Ecole Jacques Lecoq, and with Philippe Gaulier and Monika Pagneux. For Complicite: *The Caucasian Chalk Circle, The Visit, Help! I'm Alive, Burning Ambition* (BBC2) and the original production of *The Street of Crocodiles*. Other theatre: *Much Ado About Nothing* (Royal Exchange Manchester), *Epitaph for the Whales* (Gate Theatre), *Arsenic and Old Lace* (Lyceum Edinburgh), *A Better Day* (Stratford Theatre Royal), *India Song* (Theatr Clwyd), *The Jungle Book* (Young Vic), *Ay! Carmela!* (Contact Theatre Manchester), Purcell's *The Faerie Queen* (QEH). Director: *Mustard Gas and Roses* (Catapult Theatre), *The Breeze* (Hoi-Polloi Theatre), *Monsieur Henri de Toulouse-Lautrec dans son Cabaret* (Third Party) and work for the aerialists Momentary Fusion. As assistant director: *The Rose Tattoo* (Theatr Clwyd) and *Behind the Green Curtains* (O'Casey Theatre Co). TV: *The Last American Lift Operator, Oranges and Lemons, Chinese Bronzes, Peter and the Wolf, Karaoke*. Clive also teaches for Complicite and internationally.

Stefan Metz
(Performer)

Trained in Switzerland and London. For Complicite: *The Three Lives of Lucie Cabrol, Anything For A Quiet Life,* the original production of *The Street of Crocodiles* and artistic collaborator on *The Caucasian Chalk Circle.* He has worked extensively in his native Switzerland. As writer/director: *Vor Dem Gesetz, Lunatics Metropolis, Small Leaps, Giant Steps* and *Informe para una academia.* Film: *Sehnsucht, Liebe, Hoffnung.*

Cesar Sarachu
(Performer)

Born in Spain. Trained at L'Ecole Jacques Lecoq, Paris and Theatre Studio, University of the Basque Country. For Complicite: the original production of *The Street of Crocodiles.* Other theatre: (in Spain) Iturri's *Gerra ez,* Cela's *Oficio de Tiniebias,* Mrozek's *Feliz*

Aconteciemiento, Jarry's *Ubu.* (in Sweden) Granit's *Camille*, Widmer's *Top Dogs* and Handke's *The Hour we knew Nothing about Each Other.* Film: *Institute Benjamenta* (Quay Brothers), *Santa Cruz, el cura guerrillero.* Television: *La cometa blanca, Café Panamá* and *Detrás dei sirimiri.*

Matthew Scurfield
(Performer)

For Complicite: the original production of *The Street of Crocodiles.* Other theatre: *Henry V, A Chaste Maid in Cheapside* (Shakespeare's Globe Theatre) where he previously was a member of the embryo company playing The Duke of Milan in their opening production of *The Two Gentlemen of Verona,* which also performed in New York. Also: *The Trial, Macbeth,* and George in *Apart From George* (RNT), *Die Fledermaus* (ENO), *A Flea in her Ear* (Old Vic), *Agamemnon, East, Greek, Hamlet,* and *Metamorphosis* (Steven Berkoff's London Theatre Group). Television: *Kavanagh QC, A Dance to the Music of Time, A Touch of Frost, Sharpe's Honour, The Young Indiana Jones Chronicles* and *Out of Hours.* Film: *Amy Foster, Black Beauty, Dakota Road, 1984* and *McVicar.*

Christopher Shutt
(Sound)

Trained at Bristol Old Vic Theatre School. Formerly Head of Sound at the Bristol Old Vic and the Royal Court Theatres. Sound designs include: for Complicite: *The Caucasian Chalk Circle, Out of a house walked a man...*, *The Visit,* the original production of *The Street of Crocodiles, The Three Lives of Lucie Cabrol, The Winter's Tale* and *My Army Parts I and II.* Other sound designs include: *Machinal, The Homecoming, Death of a Salesman, Chips with Everything* and *Not about Nightingales* for the RNT. He has also worked for the Bush, Paines Plough and Field Day Derry. Chris is currently Sound Supervisor at the Royal National Theatre.

Ásta Sighvats
(Performer)

Trained at Middlesex University. Theatre: *The Daughter of The Poet* (The Icelandic Take-away Theatre), *King Ubu* (The Gate Theatre), *The Icequeen* (Icelandic National Theatre), *Twins* (Chisenhale Dancespace). Other work includes workshops and demonstrations with John Wright and Kazuyoshi Kushida (Flying Theatre, Jiyu Gekijo).

Rae Smith
(Designer)

For Complicite: *The Visit, Help! I'm Alive, Ave Maria* and the original production of *The Street of Crocodiles.* Rae's extensive theatre credits include: *Mrs Warren's Profession, A Christmas Carol, Sarasine, The Letter, Cause Celebre* (Lyric Theatre Hammersmith), *The Weir, Some Voices* (Royal Court), *The Cocktail Party, A Midsummer*

Night's Dream (Royal Lyceum Edinburgh), *Endgame* (Donmar Warehouse), *Silence Silence Silence* (Mladinsko Theatre, Slovenia), *The Phoenician Women*, *Henry IV* (RSC), *Gormenghast* (David Glass Ensemble), *Charley's Aunt* (Royal Exchange), *Death of a Salesman* (West Yorkshire Playhouse), *The Europeans* (Wrestling School) and *Wise Guy Scapino*. Opera: *Don Giovanni* (Welsh National Opera), *The Magic Flute* (Opera North), *Shameless* (Opera Circus) and *The Maids* (Lyric Hammersmith). Rae directed and designed *Lucky* (David Glass Ensemble), *Mysteria* (RSC) and *Terminator* (RNT Studio) and has also received two design awards for working sabbaticals in Indonesia and Japan.

Gemma Swallow
(Production Management)

Gemma began her career in administration at The Belfast Festival and subsequently moved to Scotland to work in stage management. After three and a half years as Production Manager for 7:84 Theatre Company she moved to London where she worked as a freelance Stage and Production Manager with the Young Vic, RNT Education Department and Opera Factory. For Complicite: *The Chairs*, *The Caucasian Chalk Circle*, *The Three Lives of Lucie Cabrol* and the original production of *The Street of Crocodiles*.

Mark Wheatley
(Adaptation)

Mark worked with Complicite on *The Visit* and *Help I'm Alive!* before co-adapting *The Street of Crocodiles*, *The Three Lives of Lucie Cabrol* and *Out of a house walked a man...* with Simon McBurney and adapting *Foe*. His co-adaptation of *The Street of Crocodiles* was nominated for an Olivier Award for Best Play. Most recently Mark worked on the adaptation of John Berger's novel *To The Wedding* for BBC radio. Other work includes: *Climbing Kilimanjero* (RNT Studio). Film: *La Bas* (BBC / BFI) and *Stiletto* (BFI). He is currently working on a film for children.

Ed Wilson
(Production Management)

A Front Row Production is a recently formed partnership between Ed Wilson and designer Libby Watson offering a full range of production services from design to production and general management. Ed Wilson has a long standing relationship with The Royal Court Theatre as Production Manager. For Complicite: *The Chairs*.

Bruno Schulz: a chronology

1892 12 July: Bruno Schulz born in Drohobycz, East Galicia, a province of the Austro Hungarian Empire. His father was a Jewish shopkeeper

1902 -10 Bruno attends a school named after Emperor Francis Joseph. But he does not grow up in the dominant traditions of German-speaking Austria. Nor does he remain in the sphere of traditional Jewish culture, his parents being assimilated Jews. He never learned Yiddish; he knew German but he spoke and wrote in Polish.

1905 - 15 With his father an invalid, Bruno spends all his free time at his father's bedside.

1911-13 Bruno studies at the Academy of Art in Vienna then goes on to the University of Lvov to study Architecture.

After the First World War, Poland is created a republic. Galicia is annexed by the republic in 1921.

1915-24 Years Bruno describes as his "lost, stupid and idle youth." He spends most of his time reading and drawing.

1924 Bruno begins teaching at a local high school, his earnings supporting his mother, his sister and her son. His classes are, for Bruno, an unwelcome distraction from the main business of his life - his writings and drawings. His pupils later recall the fabulous stories he told and illustrated with a few swift lines on the board or pieces of paper.

1930 Bruno publishes a book of drawings, *The Book of Idolatory*.

1932 Bruno has a one-man show of drawings and paintings in Lvov. It is a qualified success.

1934 *Cinnamon Shops,* Bruno's first book of stories, is published to wide acclaim. It is very successful and gains him the recognition and friendships he has long desired. It also brings controversy. The headmaster of the high school forbids his pupils to read it and declares it an "abomination, a scandal that profanes the Polish language".

1937   Bruno's book, *Sanatorium under the Sign of the Hourglass*, is published with illustrations by the author. He also translates *The Trial* by Kafka.

1938   Bruno works on his masterpiece, *The Messiah*. Though various sections of it were entrusted to the safekeeping of friends, none of it, to our knowledge, has survived.

17 September 1940: The German army enters Drohobycz.
Winter 1940: The Soviet army enters Drohobycz.
1941 onwards: Drohobycz under German occupation.

1941   Bruno is forced to leave his job at the high school. He offers his services as a draughtsman to the Third Reich and is refused. He is protected by a Nazi officer, Felix Landau, as a 'useful Jew'. He paints Landau's portrait.

1942: Ghetto confinement is enforced.

1942   Bruno and a fellow Jew, a solicitor, Izydor Freidmen, are employed to catalogue books for the Nazis in order that those the Nazis consider worthwhile may be exported to Germany. Bruno's friends draw up an elaborate plan of escape.

19 November 1942: The Nazis kill 150 Jews in retaliation for the shooting of a Nazi officer.

A few days earlier, Landau had shot a Jew under the protection of a rival officer. This officer takes advantage of what later becomes known as 'Black Thursday' to search Bruno out and shoot him twice in the head. "You shot my Jew, so I shot yours."

1957   Bruno's stories are reissued in Polish and translated into German and French and begin to find an international readership.

Music

Martynov	"Come In!". Soloists: Kremer & Grindenko Cond.: Bashmet Melodiya A1000625004
Shostakovich	Scene on the Boulevard from "The Bed-Bug Suite" USSR Ministry of Culture Symphony Orchestra Cond.: Rozhdestvensky Melodiya A1000107009
L'alrante folklorique	"Pot Pourri de Mirdita" Disquas Calliar 010
Janacek	Suite for Strings - Adagio movement Suk Chamber Orchestra, Cond.: Vlach Panton A1 0954 7131
Lutoslawski	String Quartet Varsovia String Quartet Pavana OCD 328
Lutoslawski	Symphony 3 Polish Radio National Symphony Orchestra Cond.: Wir Polskia Nagraina PNCD 044
Schnittke	Concerto Grosso 1 LSO. Soloist: Kremer & Grindenko, Cond.: Rozhdestvensky RCA GD 60957
Schnittke	Concerto Grosso 2. Soloists: Kagan/Gutman USSR Ministry of Culture Symphony Orchestra Cond.: Rozhdestvensky Melodiya SUCD 10 00068
Schnittke	Concerto Grosso 3. Soloists: Brautigam/Liberman/van Zweden Royal Concertgebouw Orchestra, Cond.: Chailly Decca 430 698-2

Note on the music

The Tango, which was written to exploit the musical talents of the whole company and especially the violin playing of Stefan Metz, was loosely adapted from the Tango in Alfred Shnittke's Concerto Grosso 1. The extract from Handel's **Messiah**, ("Worthy is the Lamb", the slow introduction to the work's final chorus) was freely adapted to suit the specific voices in the Company. [Gerard McBurney]

Theatre de Complicite

Theatre de Complicite ignore frontiers and cross them without official papers [John Berger]

Founded in 1983, Theatre de Complicite is a unique theatrical enterprise. An association of theatre artists with a strong sense of ensemble, Complicite brings together performers from all over the world. The only constant is the company's continuing evolution. In total, Complicite has created more than 26 productions, touring to over 180 cities in 41 countries over 4 continents. The company has won more than 25 major international awards. Recent work includes:

*   *The Chairs* (1997/8) by Eugène Ionesco, in a new translation by Martin Crimp. This widely acclaimed production, directed by Simon McBurney, was a co-production with the Royal Court Theatre. It toured England, playing a sell-out London season before going on to Broadway where it was nominated for six Drama Desk Awards and six Tonys. Geraldine McEwan won a Time Out Theatre Award and the TMA/Barclays Theatre Award for Best Actress for her role as the Old Woman.

*   *To The Wedding*, (1997) based on the novel by John Berger, adapted by Simon McBurney, John Berger and Mark Wheatley. Complicite's first radio play, co-produced with Penumbra Productions, was broadcast on BBC Radio 3 in November 1997.

*   *The Caucasian Chalk Circle* (1997) by Bertolt Brecht in a new translation by Frank McGuinness. Directed by Simon McBurney (winner of an Olivier Award), this collaboration with the Royal National Theatre played the Olivier Theatre before touring England. Complicite subsequently became the first UK company to perform Brecht's work at the Berliner Ensemble.

*   *The Three Lives of Lucie Cabrol* (1994/6) based on a story by John Berger. This production opened the Manchester City of Drama Festival, went on to tour England and play two sell-out London seasons. It also toured all over the world, winning 11 major international awards.

Theatre de Complicite Education

Education - of ourselves, our colleagues and the next generation of theatre makers - is at the heart of Complicite's work.
[Simon McBurney]

Complicite's involvement with Education work can be traced back beyond the company's formation in 1983 to the influence that teachers such as Jacques Lecoq, Monika Pagneux and Philippe Gaulier had on its founder members. Complicite's Artistic Director, Simon McBurney, describes it as "*a continuously evolving process - the process of learning.*"

Today, Complicite's Education work is wide and varied, but with one simple aim: to enable participants to throw away received, mechanical ideas and become aware of the potential of their own creativity. There is no Complicite "method". All of our work is about collaborating - and our Education programme is a central part of that concern.

We work with a wide range of groups, encompassing people of varying abilities, in a number of different ways. This can mean anything from post-show talks (open to everyone, there are three during the West End run of *The Street of Crocodiles*), through projects in prisons, to long-term relationships with schools. In the last three years, we have held a free, large scale lecture demonstration at the Royal National Theatre (based around *The Caucasian Chalk Circle*), worked with 16-25 year olds as part of the LWT Talent Challenge in Islington, as well as undertaking an innovative residency at Crown Woods School in Eltham, working on a production of *The Three Lives of Lucie Cabrol* with Sixth Form students.

What Complicite's Education programme can offer you:

Post-show talks

- Open workshops (for performers, drama students and teachers)
- Talks and workshops
- Information packs on Complicite productions
- Teaching residencies

We are always looking for new ways to develop our Education work. If you would like to become involved, or for further information, contact Kate Sparshatt on 0171 700 0233.

ROYAL NATIONAL THEATRE

NT Royal
National
Theatre

The Street of Crocodiles was first staged as a co-production with the Royal National Theatre, and opened in the National's Cottesloe Theatre on 13 August 1992.

The National, under the direction of Trevor Nunn, is a theatre for the whole nation, performing to all age groups from all communities, including the very young and those who have had no experience of theatre before. In its unique three-auditorium South Bank home, it offers the widest possible range of plays, both old and new, presented in repertoire, six days a week throughout the year, to the highest standards. It also tours each year, throughout the country and overseas, and hosts work from other countries, while engaging in education work in schools, and training and development in its Studio, to celebrate our country's unrivalled contribution to world theatre and to continue that tradition for succeeding generations.

Current and future repertoire on the South Bank includes two classics to introduce a new ensemble of actors at the NT: Shakespeare's *Troilus and Cressida* and Voltaire's *Candide*, with music by Leonard Benstein and book by Hugh Wheeler, as well as Harold Pinter's *Betrayal*, J M Barrie's *Peter Pan*; and new plays: Hanif Kureishi's *Sleep With Me*, Jonathan Harvey's *Guiding Star* (in a co-production with the Everyman Theatre, Liverpool) and Nick Darke's *The Riot* (in a co-production with Kneehigh from Cornwall), as well as Alan Ayckbourn's new version of Ostrovsky's *The Forest*.

The National is also hosting visits from The Abbey Theatre, Dublin in March with Boucicault's *The Colleen Bawn* and from Robert Lepage in April with *Geometry of Miracles*.

Work from the National can be seen elsewhere: in London J B Priestley's *An Inspector Calls* is at the Garrick, Tom Stoppard's *The Invention of Love* at the Theatre Royal, Haymarket, Rodgers & Hammerstein's *Oklahoma!* at the Lyceum, and Michael Frayn's *Copenhagen* at the Duchess. In New York, Tennessee Williams' *Not About Nightingales* is at the Circle in the Square, Patrick Marber's *Closer* opens at the Music Box in March, and David Hare's *Amy's View* will be there in the spring. Terry Johnson's *Cleo Camping, Emmanuelle and Dick* is on a major UK tour from January to March.

Apart from its main productions, the National offers all kinds of other events and services: short early-evening Platform performances; outdoor entertainment; work for children and education work; exhibitions; live foyer music; bookshops; backstage tours; a restaurant; cafés, bars and buffets; and a car park.

Royal National Theatre
South Bank
London SE1 9PX

Box Office (0171) 452 3000
Information (0171) 452 3400
Website: www.nt-online.org

Registered Charity No. 224223

Chairman of the Board
Sir Christopher Hogg

Director of the Royal National Theatre
Trevor Nunn

Executive Director
Genista McIntosh

Funded by the Arts Council of England

Note on the script

The present version of this script has been developed steadily since the project of *The Street of Crocodiles* began at the Royal National Theatre Studio in 1991. Eight years after the journey began, it is still migrating, developing and changing. Along with the original cast, we have included in this volume a list of people who have been part of that journey; most especially Jacob Schulz, Bruno's nephew, who died in 1997 and to whom this text is dedicated. For us Jacob formed the link between the present and the living past.

The script originated with the short stories of Bruno Schulz, collected in two volumes entitled *Cinnamon Shops* and *Sanatorium Under The Sign Of The Hourglass*. Because they deviate from the normal rules of narrative and eschew superficial drama, our process was as much one of invention as adaptation (to this end, we have included quotations which will point the reader to the textual inspiration at the origin of each scene). Our process involved not only the writing of original dialogue (as with any play) but also the lifting of text direct from the stories (and from Schulz's letters and essays). We used descriptions of him given to us by Jacob. We worked on improvisations in which the actors played out the process of memory which lies at the heart of all his stories. We recreated the atmosphere of his times and the mechanism of his dreams. We investigated the rhythm of his nightmares and his intense engagement with his beloved and despised solitude.

If you had opened the door of the rehearsal room when we first began you might have thought you were in a prop maker's workshop, a second-hand clothes store, or even a hallucinatory jam session, with the participants playing desks instead of drums and dancing with coats instead of partners. We used anything which came to hand to find a landmark and open up directions in which to travel. We read the stories over and over, improvised and argued. We went up blind alleys, losing ourselves in Schulz's vast imaginative landscapes and the mazes of his fantasy. For to spend time in his company turns your head (*'Dizzy with light, we dip into the enormous book of holidays, its pages scented with the sweet melting pulp of golden pears'*). The sensuality of his writing captures those long forgotten smells from the past, with an imagination that can transform gazing at a stamp album into a religious trauma (*'Canada, Honduras, Nicaragua, Abracadabra, Hipporabundia . . . I at last understood you, Oh God!'*).

So, this book is more the record of a process than a text for performance; a map rather than a play. A play is a place which demands to be inhabited; both origin and destination, linked by a clearly determined path. A map indicates the landscape, suggests a multitude of directions, but does not dictate which one you should take. A map, however beautiful, is a guide not a site. If you wish to visit the site yourself, pick up Schulz's books. And travel.

Simon McBurney and Mark Wheatley,
January 1999

The Street of Crocodiles

The Street of Crocodiles, a co-production by Theatre de Complicite and the Royal National Theatre, was first performed at the Cottesloe Theatre, Royal National Theatre, on 6 August, 1992. It toured extensively until 1994 to Australia, Canada, France, Germany, Hungary, Iceland, Ireland, Israel, Lithuania, Poland, Romania, Russia, Spain, Switzerland and all over the UK. The cast was as follows:

Joseph	Cesar Sarachu
The Father (Jacob)	Matthew Scurfield
The Mother (Henrietta)	Annabel Arden

The Family

Uncle Charles	Clive Mendus
Agatha	Joyce Henderson
Cousin Emil	Antonio Gil Martinez

The Maids

Adela	Lilo Baur
Maria	Hayley Carmichael

The Shop Assistants

Theodore	Eric Mallett
Leon	Stefan Metz

Production Manager and Lighting Paule Constable
Company Stage Manager Gemma Swallow
Costume Supervisor Johanna Coe
Sound Operator John Mackinnon
Technical Stage Manager Ian Richards

Thanks to all those who have contributed to the production over the years: Simon Auton, Sophie Brech, Dave Ball, Philip Carter, Nobby Clark, Claudia Courtis, Susan Croft, Judith Edgely, Pamela Ferris, Sue Gibbs, Gregory Gudgeon, Paddy Hamilton, Sue Higginson & the RNT Studio, Christian Huffman, Sarah-Jane Hughes, Johnny Hutch, Helena Kaut-Howson, Michael Kennedy, Irene

Kozica, Jacek Laskowski, Helen Lewis, Peter Lewis, Gerard McBurney, Richard McDougall, Pete McPhail, Rosa Maggiora, Marcello Magni, Jane Martin, Nadia Morgan, Oxford Museum of Modern Art, Naomi Parker, Picador Books, Marek Podostolski, The Polish Cultural Institute, Quay Brothers, Catherine Reiser, Lorraine Richards, Martin Riley, Richard Rudznicki, Red Saunders, Danusia Stok, Steve Wald, Russell Warren-Fisher, Octavia Wiseman, Ray Wolf.

Note

As many of the actors were from different countries, you will find in the script that they speak in their own languages.

The quotations from Bruno Schulz's work come from *The Collected Works of Bruno Schulz*, published by Picador.

Prologue

The sorting of books

As a Jew, I was assigned by the Drohobycz Judenrat to work in a library under Gestapo authority, and so was Schulz. This was a depository made up of all public and the major private libraries ... the books were to be catalogued or committed to destruction by Schulz and myself. *Letter to Jerzy Ficowksi from Tadeusz Lubowiecki, Gilwice, 1949.*

A warehouse on the outskirts of Drohobycz in Poland. 19 November 1942. Through the half dark, piles of discarded books are highlighted by spotlights.

The sound of dripping water as the audience enter the mist-filled auditorium.

Joseph *enters USL double doors. He takes off his coat and hangs it on the back wall. As he crosses DSR he looks at the bucket to see where the dripping is coming from. Exits DSR double doors.*

Voice *(off)* He du, komm her! Sortier die neue Ladung Bücher und schmeiss den Schund weg!

Joseph *(off)* Ja, ja . . .

Voice *(off)* Los, los, beweg dich!

Joseph *returns with books pushed in a packing case with wheels. He is sorting and cataloguing books. He has a pen and a sheaf of bookmarks. He writes on them and puts them in the books that are to be kept. These he takes up the ladder left and places in a row. The others he drops on the floor. One book he holds longer than others as if reluctant to commit it to destruction.*

Voice *(off)* Ja, das ist die letzte Ladung . . . die letzte, hab' ich gesagt!

Joseph *drops the book in his fright and then carries on the sorting. He finds another book particularly appealing. He is unable to throw it away. He stops, and looks at it. Out of it falls a feather. He takes a chair DSC and begins to read.*

The sound of marching feet.

Joseph *stands and watches them pass. He sits on his chair again, opens the book again. He smells its pages.*

Music.

Part One: Act of Remembrance

1 The summoning of the past

Somewhere in the dawn of childhood was The Book; the wind
would rustle through its pages and the pictures would rise. Page
after page floated in the air and gently saturated the landscape
with brightness. *The Book*

The cast gradually appear on stage as if called up by **Joseph***'s
imagination. One of* **Father***'s assistants,* **Theodore***, walks down
the wall perpendicular to the audience, pauses to take his hat and looks
up as, out of the bucket, his twin assistant,* **Leon***, appears – wet and
dripping. Having struggled out of the small bucket, he picks it up.
There is no trace of where he has come from.* **Maria** *emerges from the
packing case of books.* **Charles, Emil** *and* **Agatha** *emerge from
behind bookcases.* **Mother***, swathed in cloth, shuffles forward on her
knees with a book covered in a shawl. At a signal, they all produce
books in their hands and look at* **Joseph***.*

Joseph   And there are rooms which are sometimes
forgotten . . .

Father (*appears*)   And there are rooms which are
sometimes forgotten. Unvisited for months on end, they
wilt, become overgrown with bricks and lost once and for all
to our memory forfeit their only claim to existence. Once,
early in the morning towards the end of winter, I visted such
a forgotten chamber. From all the crevices in the floor, from
all the mouldings, from every recess there grew slim shoots
filling the grey air with a scintillating filigree lace of leaves.
Around the bed, under the lamp, along the wardrobes
clumps of delicate trees, which high above spread their
luminous crowns, enormous white and pink flowers
blossomed among the leaves, bursting with bud before your
very eyes, and then falling apart in quick decay. And before
nightfall there is no trace left of that splendid flowering. The
whole elusive sight was a *fata morgana*, an example of the

strange make-believe of matter which had created a
semblance of life.

They all proceed and sit on chairs.

	Adela	Father	Leon	Theodore	Charles
Mother					
Maria					
Emil					
Agatha					

2 The awakening of memory

Who can understand the great and sad machinery of spring? Tree
roots want to speak, freshly starched underskirts rustle on park
benches, and stories are rejuvenated and start their plots again.
Spring

At the age of 8, Bruno's mother read to him Goethe's 'Erlkönig',
of which he said later: 'Through half-understood German, I felt
its sense and was shattered and wept deeply'. *Notes to the company
from Jacob Schulz, Bruno's nephew, June 1992*

Joseph *turns and sees them. He seems to remember these people.
They are relics of his memory, a little broken down and faded. He turns
back front and they rise one by one as if attached to him. They form the
shape of a class behind him with chairs only and sit as he sits. They
begin reciting the first lines of 'Der Erlkönig'.*

Mother
Wer reitet so spät durch Nacht und Wind?

All
Es ist der Vater mit seinem Kind.

Agatha
Er hat den Knaben wohl in dem Arm

Maria
Er fasst ihn sicher . . .

Adela
 . . . er halt ihn warm.

Joseph *looks behind him. He is surprised to see these people. He looks away. They laugh and form themselves into little groups, as if at tables in an open-air café courtyard. He looks back. These are the groups behind him:* **Agatha**, **Charles** *and* **Emil** *left.* **Leon**, **Theodore** *and* **Adela** *right.* **Mother** *and* **Father** *USR.* **Maria** *centre.*

Joseph (*begins walking round them*)   Theodore? (*Goes to* **Theodore** *and takes his coat.*)

Theodore   Leon! Psst! (*Gets up.*) **Leon** (*Follows him.*)

Joseph   Leon?

They cross to **Emil** *and take his coat.* **Joseph** *watches them.*

Adela (*calls from behind* **Joseph***'s back*)   Joseph!

Joseph   Adela?

Adela   My God, Joseph, you're as thin as a rake.

Joseph *turns back to* **Leon** *and* **Theodore** *as he hears them laugh and sees . . .*

Joseph   Emil?

Emil   Hombre Joseph! Pero que allegria, chico! How wonderful to see you . . . (*He takes* **Joseph** *centre stage, behind his chair.*) You've changed, you're a man now! Un hombre! Joseph did I ever tell you what I saw in Madagascar? (*Takes him behind the chairs of* **Charles** *and* **Agatha**.*) In Madagascar I found these photos; fotografias de chicas desnuditas.

Agatha *tries to look.* **Emil** *points to distract her attention.*

Mira qué tetitas. Son las chicas de Madagas-car. (*His voice cracks on the last syllable. He tries again.*) Madagas-car. (*Same result.*)

Charles *tries to help by tuning the syllable to the highest note of the banjo.*

Madgas-*car*. (*Same result. More tuning.*) -car-car-car . . . (*Still the voice cracks.*)

Charles *has a new idea. He plays the four strings of the banjo to try and achieve the desired result.*

Emil (*tries to sing it*) Mad-da-gas-car (*Same result.*) -car-car-car . . . (*Shakes his head.*)

Father   Joseph! How extraordinary!

Joseph   Father!

Father   Even these wild and spacious late winter skies are transformed . . .

The books carried by the characters begin to flutter and change into birds, gathering in a flock DSR and then crossing DSL.

. . . by the arrival of returning birds . . . look . . . look flying hither and thither within the lap of eternal matter.

The birds flit around him in preventing **Joseph** *from seeing his father.*

Joseph   Oh Father, Father . . . Mother!

Mother   Joseph . . . Spring!

The group rises and puts chairs above their heads. We are in a wood.

The sound of birds.

Mother   What is it in the air of a spring dusk? Old trees regain their sweetness and wake up their twigs and yet there are so many whispers which lie buried underground and are forgotten. Who can understand that great and sad machinery of spring? The tree roots want to speak, memories awake, ah Joseph, freshly starched underskirts and new silk stockings rustle on park benches, their stories are rejuvenated and start their plots again. But others remain unborn and beautiful spring lives vicariously on the rejected lives of unborn tales.

Mother *has disappeared.*

Joseph   Mother, Mother . . .

Maria *appears coming DSL to stand in front of* **Joseph**.

Joseph (*goes to* **Maria**. *He does not know what to say.*)
Spring!

There is a shocked intake of breath from the wood. They raise their chairs.

Maria   Yes.

The chairs breathe out. They descend in a kind of relief. The ice has been broken.

Joseph   The stars . . . look, a shooting star!

Maria *brings out half a plate and shows it to him.*

Joseph   The moon!

Maria   No!

Joseph   Yes!

Maria   No! I'm looking for my other half. (*She indicates the other half of the plate.*)

Joseph (*he doesn't have it*)   Well . . . I'm sorry.

Maria *gets up and runs round the wood.*

Joseph (*following her*)   Hey, señorita, hey, señorita, please wait! Wait!

Maria *stops by* **Adela** *and takes her chair.* **Joseph** *pursues* **Adela**. **Adela** *stops and turns on him.*

Adela   Joseph!

Joseph   Adela?

Adela   Joseph, what are you doing out so late?

Joseph (*he is confused*)   Adela? Adela?

He stops and touches one of the trees. It falls. The other trees fall.

Joseph   My God, these people.

Maria (*stands up*)   Joseph.

Joseph   Hey señorita!

*Everyone stands up quickly and **Maria** continues to run round.*

Mother   Joseph, look! The moon! The moon!

Maria *picks up the group as she goes.*

Joseph   Yes, the moon, Mother!

The group stops DSR.

Charles   Joseph, the stars!

Joseph   Yes, the stars!

Leon   Ist das nicht wunderschön?

*The group run through **Joseph** USL. **Joseph** pursues **Maria** and grabs her. Her coat comes off and she disappears into the group.*

Joseph   Señorita, please tell me, what's your name?

*The group cross around **Joseph** to DSR and disappear.*

Agatha/Group   Joseph!

Joseph *strokes the coat with his face. The vision has disappeared but the coat tells him it was more than an imagining. He places it in the packing case and goes back to his book DSC. He looks into his book and up again.*

Part Two: The Age of Genius

1 The class

Dear and respected friend . . . School today is not the school of an earlier day . . . teaching a likeable gang of twenty-six boys equipped with hammers, saws and planes, is an honourable struggle, and the violent and desperate measures of intimidation I must resort to in order to keep them in check fill me with disgust.
Extract from a letter from Bruno Schulz to Waclaw Czarski, Chief Editor of Tygodnik Illustrowany (Polish Illustrated Weekly) Winter 1934/35

I am very much worn out by school – I now teach in grade school – I wish I could get on without a position and live for my writing alone. *Letter to Romana Halpern, Drohobycz, 1936*

There is no dead matter. Lifelessness, Emil, is only a disguise behind which lie unknown forms of life. Wood is alive.
Tailor's Dummies

The USL double doors fly open. The class are there cramming the doorway with desks and chairs. As excited children, they shake their way to CS and place themselves in a classroom formation.

Father	Mother	Charles
Two assistants	Maria	Agatha
Adela	Joseph	Emil

Joseph (*not sure what he is supposed to teach today*) Today's class is . . . (*He goes to the empty crate and looks into it.*) Today's class is . . . woodwork!

He takes wood from the crate and goes round the class distributing it. The class have their woodworking tools in their desks. They get them out and begin working as he goes round.

Emil.

Emil China, Guatemala and Madagascar . . .

Joseph Very good, Emil . . . Agatha.

Agatha *drops her piece of wood.*

Joseph   Be careful Agatha.

Agatha   Careful. (*She drops the piece of wood again.*)

Joseph   Agatha, careful.

Agatha   Careful.

Joseph   Maria . . . Maria. Where are your tools? Your tools!

Agatha *starts to bang on her desk.*

Joseph   Agatha!

Agatha   Just a little bit more.

This annoys **Emil** *so much, he decides to help* **Agatha** *with her banging.*

Emil   Like this! (*Shows her by banging with his own hammer.*)

The desk collapses. **Emil**, *mortified returns to his own desk.*

Agatha   Careful!

Joseph   Agatha, Emil what are you doing?

Emil   Rabbit brain!

Joseph   Quiet please. Go and get another desk! Hurry up! And be quiet Emil, please.

Emil *and* **Agatha** *exit to get another desk.* **Charles** *stabs the piece of wood* **Joseph** *puts down in front of him.*

Adela   Maria . . . cigarette

Joseph   Adela, quiet please . . . quiet

Leon *and* **Theodore** *play an imaginary violin and applaud.*
Adela *pushes them over.* **Joseph** *is losing control.* **Adela** *tickles* **Father. Joseph** *scolds her and sends her back to her seat.*

Adela, would you be so kind as to take your piece of wood please?

Adela *pushes the wood away from her teacher.*

Adela.

He touches her on the cheek. It is the first sign of his fascination with her. He goes on to the next desk. **Theodore** *and* **Leon** *pretend to play dead.*

Joseph   Leon . . . Theodore . . . Henrietta . . . (*gives wood to Father*) and Jacob!

Father   Crucified timbers! Who knows how many suffering, crippled forms of life there are? Such as the artificially created lives of chests and tables quickly nailed together. Lifelessness, Emil, is only a disguise within which lie unknown forms of life. Yes! Wood is alive. Wood is alive!

Emil's *wood, which he has dropped onto the floor, leaps back into his hands. Everyone else wants to try this out. Wood and tools and chairs fall everywhere.*

Mother (*standing on her chair*)   Somebody shut him up! Somebody shut him up!

Father   How much ancient suffering is there in the varnished grain of our old familiar wardrobes?

Joseph   Jacob, Jacob, please be quiet and sit down. Jacob! Let's work, please. Very good, Charles. That's it.

He indicates to **Maria** *to put her coat away. He then goes to* **Adela**'s *desk and oversees some work between* **Theodore** *and* **Leon**. *They bang on one end of a piece of wood. The other falls off. Meanwhile, USC,* **Mother** *and* **Charles** *nail* **Father**'s *hand to some wood.*

Oh my God, Jacob, show me your hand.

Father *puts his hand behind his back. When he brings it out, the nail has gone. Everyone is playing tricks on* **Joseph**.

Father   How much ancient suffering is there . . .

Joseph   Jacob . . . Henrietta you should know better . . . (*He goes round the class settling them down. He finds* **Charles** *at*

Agatha's *desk*.) Charles what are you doing there? But your place is here. (*He gives up.*)

Emil *raises his hand.*

Joseph   Yes, Emil.

Emil   Madagascar and Hipporabundia!

Joseph   Very good Emil, thank you. (*Indicates his chair to sit down.*)

Emil   Guatemala!

Joseph   Very good, Emil.

Emil   Hipporabundia!

Joseph   Emil, please sit down.

Emil   Uganda, Tanganika and Mozambique!

Joseph   Emil, please . . .

Emil   Paraguay, Uruguay, Venezuela!

Joseph   EMIL!

Emil *sits down contritely.* **Joseph** *sits down.* **Theodore** *and* **Leon** *play with* **Adela**, *singing a little song, to the tune of 'Daisy, Daisy'.*

Assistants
   Adela, Adela, give us your answer do.

Joseph   Shh . . . Shhhh (*Begins to go to sleep.*)

Assistants (*quietly*)
   We're half crazy, all for the love of you.
   It won't be a stylish marriage,
   We can't afford the carriage,
   But we'll look sweet upon the seat
   Of a bicycle made for two.

Adela *has had enough. She turns and lifts her skirt at them. She gets a glass out of her desk and goes to the tap.* **Joseph** *goes to sleep DSC.*

Charles   Agatha . . . (*Blows sawdust in* **Agatha***'s face.*)

Agatha   Charles . . . (*Takes a hammer and hits his thumb.*)

Charles *puts up his hand to appeal to* **Joseph** *at this injustice.*
Joseph *does not respond.* **Adela***, at the tap drinking water, notices*
Joseph *is asleep. She creeps back to her desk. She drops a piece of*
wood to see if it will wake him up. The whole class follows suit,
banging furiously. **Joseph** *remains asleep. The class hatch a plan.*
Charles *makes a wooden spoon with* **Leon** *and* **Theodore***. He*
leads the sleeping **Joseph** *round the classroom in a dance of death, the*
class providing the rhythmical accompaniment. **Joseph** *ends by*
standing on a chair in the middle of the room. **Agatha** *'shoots' him.*
Joseph *staggers to his chair. The class approach, tapping a sinister*
rhythm. He wakes up. He looks round at the class to see if it was a
dream. The class behave as if everything were normal. But they are now
out of control. They start shifting around the desks. **Joseph** *cannot*
bring them back to their original positions. They suddenly stop.
Joseph *looks at Jacob. He realises that it is his* **Father***.*

Father   How much ancient suffering is there in the
varnished grain of our old familiar wardrobes?

Joseph   Father –

Unable to believe this dreamlike transformation, he goes to the tap to
put cold water on his face.

2 The shop of childhood memory

Childhood . . . oh that invasion of brightness, that blissful spring,
oh, Father . . . *The Book*

The class move their desks around as they work gradually forming them
into a shop counter, ready for the next scene. **Joseph** *looks up from*
the tap. The noise stops and the desks, in a line, conceal the cast. The
tap drips. He turns back to it and stops it. He moves towards the desks,
looking at his **Father***. As he does so, a bell rings. It is the door to the*
shop. He tries opening the imaginary door. A bell rings again. He
walks into the shop and sees it is his **Father***'s shop which he*
remembers from his earliest childhood. He goes to his **Father***, pushing*
down all the desk lids. This reveals the group in various stages of sleep.

The group move to the back of the stage, except for **Father**, *who is at the end of the table.*

At noon, the shop experienced a momentary pause and relaxation: the hour of the afternoon siesta . . . the shop assistants abandoned themselves for a moment to the delights of yawning and turned somersaults on the bales of cloth. *The Dead Season*

Joseph *watches the shop inhabitants in a playful mood. The shop is sleeping.*

Joseph (*blows on his* **Father**'s *head*)   Father.

The sound of birds flapping. **Father** *wakes momentarily.*

Father   Genus avium, bubus alba. (*He makes the hoot of an owl.*)

Joseph (*tries to imitate him, unsuccessfully. He runs to his* **Mother**.) Mother. (*He finds an egg in her hair.*)

Mother (*wakes momentarily*)   . . . Egyptian cotton white lilac twenty-five pillow cases which I ordered from Warsaw and nobody ever knows if they're going to deliver them on a Thursday or a Friday. Ah, there you are !

Joseph *runs to the roll of cloth SL and touches it. He runs to the back of the shop and touches the coats there. The coats emit sounds of their previous owners. He smells* **Adela.** *She yawns and stretches in her slumber.*

Father (*runs to the back, still asleep*) June, July, September . . . Where's August? I can't find August!

Theodore *runs to the front and back again. He and* **Leon** *come to the front and fall on the counter in front of* **Father**, *who takes letters from his hand and pushes the assistants towards* **Mother**.

Father   Thank you.

Adela's *unsuccessful cleaning of the counter is blocked by* **Mother**'s *head.* **Leon** *and* **Theodore** *lift* **Mother**'s *head for* **Adela** *to clean. The sound of* **Mother** *laughing. The assistants lie on the counter again, holding their rolls of cloth.* **Adela** *goes back to the back wall.*

3 Father's beautiful shop

It was the age of electricity and mechanics and a whole swarm of
inventions was showered on the world by the resourcefulness of
human genius . . . in every house electric bells were installed.
The Comet

Joseph   Wake up . . . wake up. (*Bangs one of the desk lids.*)

Assistants *unroll two lengths of cloth, which hurtle downstage.*
Father *and* **Mother** *awake.* **Maria**, **Agatha**, **Emil** *and*
Charles *stand up like dummies USL.*

Father   The cloth, the cloth.

Mother   Yes indeed, the cloth.

Father   Who among the present generation of textile
merchants remembers the good traditions of their ancient
art? Who remembers, boys, that if you fold the cloth
according to the principles it will emit a sound like a
descending scale?

Mother   Like a descending scale

Father   At the touch of a finger, Theodore.

Mother   Not even a finger, Jacob.

Father   Not even a finger.

Mother   Not even a – boys, boys, open the shop !

Music from light entertainment radio of the era.

Assistants *leave the cloth and* **Father** *and run to the back wall.*
They grab **Adela** *and lift her onto the counter.* **Joseph** *joins in.*

Joseph   Adela, open the shop.

Adela *begins scrubbing the floor.* **Mother** *and* **Father** *continue a
long-running argument as they dance.* **Mother** *and the* **Assistants**
dress the dummies. **Joseph** *watches* **Adela** *from behind a coat.*
Father *climbs to his office on the back wall.* **Joseph** *rolls* **Maria**,
Emil, **Agatha** *and* **Charles** *out of the shop to become shoppers
USL.* **Leon** *and* **Theodore** *push a pole through* **Adela**'s *legs and*

carry her on it. **Father** *whistles at them. The shoppers are coming.*
They panic to find the door handle and bell. Coming to the shop, **Emil**
chatters to **Charles** *and* **Agatha** *about what they are going to buy.*

Emil   Veréis qué tienda tan meravillosa. La más moderna.
Os voy a enseñar los avances de la técnica, el futuro, un
timbre eléctrico, lo automático, con dinero se puede todo!
(*Indicates the assistants' bell. Standing outside the shop he manages to*
get hold of the door handle, which the **Assistants** *have been*
annoyingly playing with.) Aha!

Emil, Charles *and* **Agatha** *sweep in, and stand DSR.*

Charles, Agatha, the mystery of electricity. It rings by itself.

Agatha   Really?

Charles   I don't believe it!

Emil   You will . . . brrrrrrr (*Makes sound of bell.*) . . .
Automático.

They sweep up to the counter.

Good morning!

Assistants   Djin Dobre!

Emil   Now listen . . . I have come with my friends to buy
. . . para comprar un timbro eléctrico.

Maria, *the little orange one, slips in front of* **Emil** *to try and buy*
something first.

Emil   Señorita, se ha colado usted . . .

Maria *takes no notice.*

Emil   Señorita, estaba yo primero . . .

Maria *continues to take no notice,* **Emil** *gives up temporarily.*

Here follows a whole number of **Maria** *attempting to communicate*
with **Joseph** *and show him her plate. The* **Assistants** *think*
Maria *wants to buy something and deliberately play games with her,*
seizing her plate and pretending to match it with all sorts of absurd

*objects, finishing with a real plate which they smash. She snatches back
her precious half plate and runs away. This is **Emil**'s chance to get
in. He takes it.*

Emil   Vamos aver por favor, despáchenme, que no tengo
toda la mañana. Good morning, now listen. Good Morning!

*He finally has the attention of the **Assistants**.*

Assistants   Djin Dobre!

Emil   Djin Dobre! . . . Herr Jacob?

Assistants (*turning to **Mother***)   Herr Jacob?

Mother   Komm später.

Assistants   Komm später!

Emil   Well never mind, now listen. Yo lo que quiero es un
timbre eléctrico; 'The mystery of electricity, it rings by
itself'. (*He reads from the newspaper.*) 'El simbolo del progresso,
la téchnica y lo automático, aquí para mis amigos . . .'

Charles   We're hoping for a demonstration.

Agatha   Yes. And I would like to be the one to pay for it.
No, no I insist . . .

*Here the **Assistants** who have understood nothing, play a joke on
Agatha and give her a bone instead of the bell. The bone routine then
ensues. Being thrown back and forth until . . .*

Emil   Agatha! Charles, Charles, you explain, Charles,
Charles, they don't understand. Listen . . .

Charles   Yes, it's really very simple. All my friend is
asking for is . . .

Assistants   Capeluche?

*They get out a couple of top hats. They start putting them on
Charles' and **Emil**'s head. Confusion reigns. They speak
simultaneously.*

Charles   No, no, no, listen, you didn't understand. I don't want a hat. I want . . . where is my hat . . . what? (*Hits himself over the head with a bone.*) Give me my hat, EMIL!!

Emil   No, no, no, no, I don't want a capeluche. What I want is one of these. (*Indicates newspaper.*) No, no, what are you doing What . . . no . . . no . . . what . . . no . . . BASTA!! We'll try again! Now listen . . .

Passing in front of the counter as they change sides, he gets given the bone; he smells it and it makes him sneeze.

Emil   Atchooo . . . (*Throws the bone away.*) Now listen . . . yo lo que quiero es un timbre eléctrico . . . An electric bell!

Charles   Voilà!

Emil   Se le da al botoncito, core por un circuito eléctrico galvanizado y prrrrrrrrr! Suena dentro de la casa, automático!

Assistants *shake a pair of fake castanets at him.*

No, no, no, no. Es automatico. Que Se le da al botoncito, core por un circuito electrico galvanizado y prrrrrrrrr! Atchoo!!!! (*Looks for handkerchief from* **Agatha** *and* **Charles**.) No tiene un handkerchief por favor? No? Enfin . . . Que Se le da al botoncito, corre poor un circuito electrico galvanizado y prrrrrrrrr! Atchoo!!!!

This time the **Assistants** *have put his coat sleeve under his nose and* **Emil** *has had enough of their fooling around.*

Oiga! Pero, que me estan manchando el abrigo nuevo de mocos! Charles! Pero esto es disgusting; me están faltando al respecto. Que se la están buscando. Que yo se boxe, que yo se boxe, que la aprendí en Paris, que le doy, que le doy, que soy un campeón, hop, hop. What are you doing? You've ruined my new coat . . . Charles . . . Look . . . this is disgusting. I see . . . I see . . . you are looking for trouble!

Don't think I haven't noticed! Que se la están buscando. Que yo se boxe, que la aprendí in Paris, que le doy, que.

Emil *and the* **Assistants** *start to pretend to fight. Chaos.*

> An electric bell is an ordinary mystification. The fabric of life can be found within the weave of a cloth. *The Comet*

Jacob (*whistles from his perch*)   Good heavens, Theodore, Leon, I never knew we'd ordered so many eggs.

Emil   Hombre Jacob. At last. I have come here tranquilamente y estos señores me están faltando al respeto.

Mother   And how can we help you?

Emil   Estoy buscando un timbre eléctrico.

Father   I'm sorry?

Emil   I would like an electric bell.

Father (*comes down on a rope from his perch*)   An electric bell . . . Why?

Emil   Why? Why? Because I have to show my friends exactly how it works . . . the principles of connection, electricity . . .

Father (*asking for the newspaper*)   May I see? Look Joseph, an electric bell.

Emil   An electric bell.

Father   An electric bell is of course a miracle of modern science.

Emil   Is progress . . .

Father   But it is an ordinary mystification.

Emil   It is an ordinary mystifica ca ca como?

Father   Progress? Well some may call it that. It is not man who has broken into the laboratory of Nature, but Nature who uses man's ingenuity for her own purposes.

Mother   Jacob, he only wants to buy something.

Emil   Exactemente.

Father   I'm sorry. Some Indian silk perhaps . . . Egyptian cotton . . . A Royal tartan . . . a Persian cadar?

Emil   No, no, no, . . . yo no quiero un Persian cadar . . .

Jacob   No, you're right the pattern is too heavy. Allow us to show the pure white calaphony from Malabar?

Emil   No, no, no, yo no quiero un calaphony from Malabar. Hombre, yo lo que quiero es un timbre eléctrico . . . Que se le da al botoncito, core por un circuito eléctrico y prrrrrrrr. Atchoo!!!! Es automático, es progreso, moderno.

Father *takes a handkerchief from his top pocket.*

Emil   Maravilioso . . . pero yo lo que quiero un electric bell . . . Botoncito . . . Circuito . . . prrrrrrrrr Atchoo!!!! (*As he searches for a handkerchief*.) Perdón, qué tengo una alergia y no puedo hablar, perdón qué raro. Pero lo importante, es un timbre eléctrico. ¿Que hace Jacob?

Father *takes a handkerchief from his wig*. **Emil** *irritatedly snatches the handkerchief.*

Emil   Perfecto . . . Un electric bell . . . Botoncito . . . Circuito . . . prrrrrrrrr . . . Atchoo!!!! (*Underneath the action.*) Pero qué hace, qué me pica, qué dolor eléctrico rapido, Charles, Charles, una conexíon!

Father *does a magic trick.* **Emil** *shrieks and shakes as the hankerchief travels round his body.* **Charles** *removes it from his sock. General applause and amazement.*

Emil   Fantástico!

Father   An electric bell is of course a miracle of modern science, but the migration of forms is the essence of life. The fabric of life can be found within the weave of a cloth.

Emil   Cloth.

Charles/Agatha   Cloth . . .

Father   Allow us to show this with the calaphony from Malabar?

Emil   Hombre, it's not what I wanted, but if you insist . . .

Father   The true calaphony comes from the robes of the ritual dancers of Hipporabundia . . .

Emil   Hipporabundia . . .

Charles/Agatha   Hipporabundia . . .

Father   Now listen. (*He passes his hands over the cloth. It makes a ringing sound.*)

Emil (*genuinely surprised*)   An electric bell!

Charles   An electric bell.

Father   If you fold the cloth according to the principles it will emit a sound like a descending scale.

Mother   Gentlemen, my husband, a remarkable man in spite of everything, truly remarkable.

Father (*unfolds the cloth with the aid of the two* **Assistants**) This cloth pulsates with infinite possibilities that sends dull shivers through it. Indulgently acquiescent, pliable like a woman . . .

Joseph   Like a woman!

Father   It is a territory outside any law, a domain of beauty and godlike manipulation. Modern science however is transient and temporary.

The cloth begins to move. **Emil**, **Charles**, **Agatha** *and* **Maria** *move with it, apparently knocked off balance by its beauty. This rapidly leads to a dance. Behind the screen of the table-cloth the shop counter is being transformed into the dining room table.*

4 Family dinner

We lived on Market Square, in one of those dark houses with empty blind looks, so difficult to distinguish one from the other.
Visitation

The family sit round the table, in this order:

> Charles   Mother   Agatha   [empty chair]
>
> Joseph   Emil

Assistants *exit.* **Adela** *and* **Maria** *stand by the stove.*

Joseph *greets everyone at the table.*

Mother   Ah Joseph! There you are!

Joseph   I'm sorry I'm late. Cousin Emil . . . (*He tries to kiss his cousin.*)

Emil   Cheech la mano! Que ya eres un hombre! Hipporabundia and Madagascar!

Agatha   Careful!

She puts **Joseph***'s hands on her breasts. They embrace,* **Joseph** *a little uncomfortably.*

Hasn't he grown!

Joseph *embraces his mother.* **Charles** *takes a letter out of* **Joseph***'s pocket.*

Charles   Love letters?

Emil   You're a man now.

Joseph *sits.*

Noise of birds flapping in the roof.

Everybody looks up. With the exception of **Joseph** *they all remain immobile for the next scene.*

5 The maids

Maria was a woman who hired herself to housewives to scrub
floors. She was a small saffron-yellow woman, and it was with
saffron that she wiped the floors, the deal tables, the benches, and
the banisters which she had scrubbed in the homes of the poor.
August

Maria   Adela

Adela   Maria

Adela *and* **Maria**, *who is smoking a cigarette and clutching an
enormous book to her chest, walk from USR to the tap.* **Adela** *fills the
bucket with water.*

You know Maria, when I was a little girl we had no running
water.

Maria   No running water?

Adela   Water was precious.

Maria   Precious.

Adela   Yes, I was only allowed to wash myself once a week

Maria   Once a week?

Adela   Yes.

Maria   Once a week?

Adela   What?

Maria   You must have stunk Adela.

Adela   Zigorette.

Maria   Adela, that's my cigarette.

Adela   You shouldn't smoke Maria, it's very bad for your
health.

Maria   It's bad for your health.

Adela   No, your health . . .

Maria   Your health . . .

Adela/Maria   Your health . . . Your health . . . Your health . . .

Adela *puts out the cigarette in the bucket of water.*

Maria   But Adela, you said water was precious.

Adela   I say many things Maria . . . hurry up!

Maria *gives* **Adela** *her red shoes from the big book.*

Maria   But . . . Adela

Adela   Maria, carry my boots.

Maria *puts* **Adela**'s *boots inside the big book.* **Adela** *puts on her red shoes.*

Maria   Yes . . . Adela . . .

Adela   Maria, what did I just say?

Maria   Carry my boots.

Adela   Yes!

Maria   But Adela . . .

Adela   Maria . . .

Maria   Yes?

Adela   Silence is golden.

They return to the stove.

6 The table of boredom

> The days passed, the afternoons grew longer: there was nothing to do in them. A yellow monotony, an elemental boredom. We were inclined to underrate the value of Father's sovereign magic, which saved us from the lethargy of empty days and nights.
> *Tailor's Dummies*

Sound of birds flapping.

The cruet set flies in gracefully.

Mother   Ah! There you are!

Adela (*marches to the table with spoons and dishcloth*)   Oxtail soup.

Mother   Oxenswantzsuppe!

Charles   Wunderbar!

Emil   Maravilloso! Ostersoops!

Adela   Oxtail!

Emil   Oster . . . ?

Adela   OX!

Emil   Os . . . es lo que dico, Ostersoops . . . is my favourite dish. Everytime I go to Paris I insist on having this magnificent soup, because I think it is a superb soup . . .

He becomes hypnotised by **Adela***'s onanistic cleaning of the cutlery beside him.* **Adela** *registers his sexual excitement, hits him in disgust and the plates tumble out onto the table. First two from* **Emil***, then* **Agatha***, then* **Mother** *and lastly* **Charles** *who for some unknown reason brings out a bottle instead of a plate. He rectifies this quickly with two more plates.*

Sound of violent bird flapping overhead.

Feathers fall from the ceiling.

Mother   Birds! Up in the attic with Father! At great expense of time and money, Father has imported from Hamburg and Holland and zoological stations in Africa . . .

Emil   Africa . . .

Charles/Agatha   Shhh!

Mother   Rare birds' eggs, which he has set up in the attic under enormous brood hens from Belgium.

Charles   La Belgique.

Emil   Belgica.

Adela   Belgian hens. (*She holds* **Joseph**'s *head and polishes a spoon on her breast.*) Yes but the point is, we eat later and later every day.

Mother   Adela . . .

Adela *leaves the table.*

Joseph *picks up the spoon that* **Adela** *was polishing and starts to kiss it. The rest of the table is slightly taken aback at this auto-eroticism. They laugh to cover their embarrassment.*

Mother   He's trying to hatch them.

Agatha   He's trying to hatch them.

Mother   Hatch them . . .

Agatha   Hatch them . . .

They laugh together. Then they sigh. All look gloomly out front. The clock begins to tick. **Agatha**'s *fan takes the rhythm of the clock.* **Emil** *notices* **Agatha**'s *fan.*

Emil   Joseph did I ever tell you about my time in Africa . . . ? Well we were on safari in Uganda, Tanganika and Mozambique . . . Una tarde de verano muy calorosa. Qué calor, África. Cuando de pronto saliendo de la espesura se avalanzó sobre nosotros un rinoceronte. Yo se cómo son esos animales cuando se enrabietan, pero allí me quedé, haciéndole frente solo ante el peligro, los demás salieron por piernas, ha, ha, . . . Pero he aquí que un tigre, un elefante, un gorila, un hippopótamo . . . en fin manadas enteras de animales salvajes empezaron a venir; yo por supuesto, saqué mi rifle apunte y me puse a pegar tiros como un valiente y túe qué sabes que cuadro másh impresionante . . .

Emil *sees his own reflection in his cigarette case and gets distracted. He forgets completely that he is recounting an exciting story. He suddenly rediscovers his rapt audience.*

Oh, enfin . . . the whole adventure was very dangerous, very!

Mother   How very nice for you.

Agatha *laughs.*

The clock ticks. Boredom.

Charles *starts to fall asleep into his soup plate. As he hits the plate . . .*

Emil   Constantinopla!

Charles   Ah yes!

Boredom.

Now perhaps is the moment I might draw a parallel between Alexander the Great and my modest self. Alexander was susceptible to the aroma of countries. He felt as unfulfilled as I, he hungered after ever wider horizons and landscapes. There was no one who could point out his mistake. Not even Aristotle could understand him.

Father *enters from SR ladder.*

> My father, that incorrigible improvisor, that fencing master of the imagination led colourful and splendid counter-offensives of fantasy against the boredom that strangled the city. *Tailor's Dummies*

Father   The birds!

All   Jacob!

Father   Joseph, you should see the birds, the curlews have come back and the peacocks . . . eggs the colour of dreams.

Joseph   Father.

Mother   Ah Jacob, there you are!

Father   By the way Hettie, you were right, we are missing a month . . .

Mother   No, it's not missing.

Father   June, July . . . here's September, but I can't find August.

Adela *enters with soup and stands waiting to serve.*

Father (*sees* **Charles**)   I am sorry. I am concerned with this section of space which you are filling.

Charles *goes to the other end of the table and sits on the chair offered to him by* **Adela**. *She is still waiting to serve the soup.* **Father** *sits. He brings out a bird's egg.*

Father   Matter is in a state of constant fermentation. It never holds the same shape for very long. Am I to conceal from you . . .

Mother   Oh, please will somebody shut him up.

Everybody looks at **Adela** *in expectation.*

Father   No Hettie please, I must tell this story . . .

Adela *advances towards* **Father**.

Father   Adela, please.

She tickles him until he can bear it no longer. He is silent. **Adela** *has won their first battle. She raises her finger at him in warning and goes back to serve the soup. She stirs the pot of soup gently, as* **Father** *watches in fascination. She suddenly notices that* **Emil** *is getting an erotic charge off this motion. She slaps some soup in his plate, to put an end to it. She serves* **Charles**, *who is also excited by the way in which she does it. Then she goes to* **Mother**.

Mother   Und ein kleines bisschen mehr.

Adela/Mother   And a little bit more . . .

Adela *serves* **Agatha**.

Agatha   And a little bit more . . .

She doesn't get any more. **Adela** *serves* **Father** *and* **Joseph**. **Joseph** *is holding the egg.*

Adela   Joseph, stop playing with the egg, we are eating now.

Father   Very remarkable, very remarkable indeed.

Mother   Thank you Adela. Well, you must all be completely exhausted.

Charles and **Emil** *agree. Everyone settles down to eat.*

Father (*excitedly pushes his soup away*)   Am I to conceal from you . . .

Adela   Herr Jacob we are eating now.

Father   No, I must tell you this story . . . Adela please.

Adela *puts* **Father***'s soup back in front of him. He pushes it away. Repeat five times.*

Adela (*waves a spoon at him*)   No!

Everyone watches, electrified, as – very slowly – **Father** *capitulates and takes a mouthful of soup.*

Father   Wunderbar soup Adela, wunderbar.

Adela   Bon Appétit! (*Exits.*)

The meal begins. Everyone chatters loudly. **Father** *checks that* **Adela** *is no longer in the vicinity.*

Father   Am I to conceal from you . . . Emil, Charles, listen. (*He is unable to attract anybody's attention.*)

Mother *is talking to* **Agatha**. **Charles** *is listening to* **Emil**.

Father *hatches a plan. He creeps behind* **Charles** *and, while* **Charles** *is not looking, switches the cigar round, so that the lit end now faces* **Charles**' *mouth.* **Father** *nips back to his chair and awaits the result.* **Charles** *cries out in pain.*

Mother   Jacob!

Father (*takes his opportunity*)   Am I to conceal from you that my own brother, as a result of a long and incurable illness, has been gradually transformed into a bundle of rubber tubing?

Adela *returns to the table.*

Father　Can there be anything sadder than a human being changed into the rubber tube of an enema? What a disappointment for his parents. And yet the faithful love of my cousin, who used to carry him day and night on a cushion . . .

Mother　Adela!

Adela *lifts her fingers, threatening to start tickling* **Father** *again, who begins laughing at the merest suggestion.*

Father　And yet the faithful love of my cousin . . . the faithful love . . . No, no, please stop . . .

His laughing becomes painful. **Adela** *does not stop the torture.*

We need the privilege of creation . . . we need creative delights . . .

In one gesture, **Adela** *cuts off his laughter. With a second gesture, he reacts as if smacked round the face. With* **Adela**'s *third gesture (as if she were throwing something into the pot), he collapses onto his chair like a sack of potatoes. He is humiliated.*

> Adela's complexion, under the influence of the springward gravitation of the moon, became younger, acquired milky reflexes, opaline shades and the glaze of enamel. She now had the whip hand . . . *The Comet*

All begin laughing and chattering again to cover their embarrassment. **Joseph** *touches* **Father** *in sympathy.*

Father (*stands up*)　Matter doesn't make jokes. It is always full of the tragically serious.

As he begins this, the table falls silent but appears to be continuing its chatter. He sits down again. The voices of everyone at the table return. He stands again.

You may laugh, but in the wink of an eye . . .

He becomes aware that again the table has fallen silent, while appearing to continue their chatter. He is surprised, then delighted. He tries it two or three times — standing and sitting.

Matter is in a state of constant fermentation. Matter can change in an instant, Joseph. (*He takes out his magnifying glass and makes* **Joseph** *look at the table through it.*) In the wink of an eye we may no longer be who we think we are.

Emil, **Charles**, **Agatha**, **Mother**, **Maria**, **Adela**, **Leon** *and* **Theodore** *turn into birds.*

Father (*walks onto the table*)   Genus Avium . . .

The people, now birds, respond with a chorus of bird calls.

Joseph   Oh Father . . . your birds, Father.

A chorus of bird calls.

Father   Very remarkable, very remarkable indeed. This is ibis ibis, the Spanish stork. (*He points out* **Emil** *and gets down off the table.*)

Joseph   May I feed them?

Father   Of course you can feed them, Joseph. Here we have the wrens . . . (*He points out* **Adela** *and* **Maria**.)

Joseph   From England!

Father   Trogladytes, trogladytes, trogladytes . . .

Joseph (*points out* **Charles**)   Columba aquatica.

Father   Not quite Joseph, columba aquatrix.

Joseph (*points at Leon on the wall*) This is cuccus solitarius.

Father (*points at* **Theodore** *on the table*)   and this is cuccus lacteus, Joseph and here we have a . . . (*Looks at* **Agatha**.)

Joseph   A peacock!

Father   And here is a broody hen . . . (*Looks at* **Mother**.)

The birds chorus to a climaxing response. **Joseph** *takes a book and it begins to flap and fly like a bird.*

Joseph   Oh Father . . . your birds, Father.

Behind his back, in three movements, the scene dissolves back to the table.

Adela (*takes* **Joseph** *by the ear and makes him sit down.*) Joseph . . . we are eating now!

Father   Very remarkable . . .

Adela (*in warning, raising her finger*)   Herr Jacob!

Father *defies her and calls to his birds with the sound of a cuckoo.* **Adela** *raises her ladle. As she does so a piece of birdshit falls, loudly, onto the cloth. Outrage from everyone.*

Father   Theodore, Leon, this is a very remarkable stool . . . It's ibis ibis the Spanish stork!

Adela   That is the limit.

Mother   Adela, please . . .

Adela   I do not believe it, birdshit on the tablecloth . . .

Mother   I can see what it is.

Adela   No! I was not employed here to clean up birdshit . . .

Mother   I know.

Adela   Herr Jacob is getting wilder and wilder every day, now he has a bird hospital up in the attic.

Father *hides behind his ledger.*

Mother   Adela, please we'll talk . . .

Adela   No! Just look at the new tablecloth, it's completely ruined . . . and it stinks!

Mother   Adela, you are a wonderful girl.

All   Yes, wonderful . . .

Mother   Wonderful in every way, don't think of leaving us. Jacob, you must apologise, we have a problem.

Father   Yes, you're right, we do have a problem we're missing a month.

Mother   What do you mean we're missing a month?

Father   I can't account for the seasons. June, July, here's September . . . but I can't find August.

Mother It's on the calico where you left it.

Father   No I couldn't have mislaid it, you must have mislaid it.

Mother   Apologise!

Father   Adela . . .

Mother   Apologise!

Father   August, August, August . . .

Mother   That's enough! Put it with the other months.

Adela   Yes!

Mother *takes the ledger and gives it to* **Adela**. **Father** *snatches it back as she walks past.*

Adela   Herr Jacob, bring me that month!

Father   Not until you bring me August . . .

Adela   Bring it to me . . .

Father   August . . .

Adela   Bring it here . . .

Father   August . . .

Adela   Right that's it. Give it here.

The ledger is snatched by **Mother**, *passed from* **Assistant** *to* **Assistant** *and back to* **Father**. **Adela** *promptly takes it away again. The ledger takes on a life of its own, responding to* **Father**'s *transformational abilities. The ledger flies out of* **Adela**'s *hands, through the* **Assistants**, *down the table, making a big circle, ending with* **Joseph** *who returns it to* **Father**. *With everyone hanging on,* *the ledger sways to and fro, until the group is catapulted towards ledgers placed around the room.* **Adela** *is the only one unaffected. In disgust, she picks up her bucket and, with* **Maria**, *goes to the tap. The ledgers now have control of everyone. They fly DSC back up to* **Father**, *round the table, eventually ending – with the music – when* **Emil** *sits on his chair and the books fall on top of him. Adela bangs down her bucket at the tap. All watch her as she returns angrily to the stove.*

7 August

The untidy, feminine ripeness of August had expanded into enormous, impenetrable clumps of burdocks . . . with their luxurient tongues of fleshy greenery . . . a tangled thicket of grasses, weeds and thistles crackled in the fire of the afternoon. The sleeping garden was resonant with flies. *August*

Adela *bangs bucket beside the stove. With a great show of patience she opens the stove and takes out a ledger. She throws it on the table in front of the assembled company.*

Adela   August!

Father   Adela . . . (*Tries to grab the ledger.*)

Adela   Don't touch it!

Father *tries again.*

Adela   Hands off!

Joseph (*takes the book. He kisses it. He touches it with his forehead. He gives it to* **Mother**.)   August. (*He begins to open the book.*)

Mother   Ah, August . . .

Everyone looks into the book.

Mother (*continues to open the book. She stands on her chair.*)   The endless holidays . . .

Everyone looks out front as if they can see the endless holidays. **Mother** *steps onto the table. The chairs move apart mirroring the opening pages. The family group help* **Mother** *over the table.*

Mother   Days and days and days full of the sweet melting pulp of golden pears. And the ripe morello cherries that smelled so much better than they tasted. The golden squares of sunlight falling on a wooden floor. A distant chord played on a piano over and over.

She has come down the other side of the table towards the audience. **Joseph** *is sitting on* **Leon**'s *shoulders.* **Emil** *and* **Theodore** *are holding the books as if they were a set of bannisters.*

And I would walk with Joseph in Market Square. It was completely empty, you see, nobody there. And yes, yes . . . I had had a little wine . . .

The books collapse, changing from a bannister into a small seat for **Agatha***. Everyone looks towards* **Adela** *at the tap.* **Adela** *turns towards them and takes off her dress, revealing pink beneath the green.*

Ah, there you are.

Leon *and* **Theodore** *lift up the tablecloth over the heads of the seated group and place it in front of them on the ground, like a picnic napkin.* **Mother** *sits down behind it with* **Emil***,* **Charles** *and* **Agatha***, DSC.* **Maria** *puts a long parasol into a hole on the table.* **Adela** *advances towards the group, leaving her shoes on the DSL corner of the cloth. She kicks* **Theodore** *languidly out of the way. She pours* **Mother** *some raspberry syrup. It is hot.* **Adela** *sits on the cloth in front of them, with* **Maria***.* **Father** *sits just behind everyone, up on the table. He looks at* **Adela***.*

Father   How delightful and happy is the form of existence which you ladies have chosen. How beautiful and simple is the truth which is revealed by your lives. If forgetting the respect due to the Creator I were to attempt criticism of creation, I would say less matter more form. What a relief it would be for the world to lose some of its contents, just some of its contents.

A buzzing fly is swatted on the tablecloth by **Theodore***.*

Agatha   Joseph, do you remember, when we were children we used to play together. (*She stands up, taking*

Joseph *by the hand towards the tap.*) On Stryska Street, there is
a pharmacy and in the window a huge jar of raspberry juice
which they claimed could cure all summer ills. (*She tries to get
some raspberry syrup out of the tap. Nothing emerges.*)

Joseph *escapes to the group. He waves* **Emil***'s hand. Waving*
Emil*'s hand reminds* **Emil** *of the heat.*

Emil   Qué calor! Como en África. This provincial climate
is known by the experts as a chinese summer in *China* of
course . . . China . . . China . . . China . . .

(*He is unable to pronounce the word China without his voice cracking.*
Charles *helps by tuning him to his banjo. This makes* **Emil** *begin
to sing.*) China, thank you, China it is too long . . . (*Realises he
is singing and stops in embarrassment.*) hem . . . far too long. In
Alaska, for example, the summer is only this long, and then
it's finished.

Charles   Do you know why animals have horns? It is
because they have such incredible imaginations. Their
fantasies, unlike ours, emerge into the air above their heads
and take on weird unpredictable shapes . . . A sort of *idée fixe*.

Theodore *and* **Leon** *play with the iron on the cloth.* **Maria** *and*
Adela *play with the cutlery. We focus on* **Joseph***. He points*
Charles*' finger at* **Emil***'s hair.*

Charles   Excuse me.

Emil   Yes?

Charles   Is that a real wig?

Emil   And that. (*Pushes back* **Charles***' hat.*) Is that a real
bald patch?

Mother, **Agatha** *and* **Emil** *roar with laughter.* **Emil** *throws his
head back in laughter and his wig falls off. He quickly puts it back on
and stands patting* **Mother***'s hand, absolutely mortified. Joseph sees*
Adela*'s shoes and goes and lays his head beside them on the floor. He
takes one and puts it, heel down, on his face.* **Adela** *comes to retrieve*

it. The **Assistants** *begin to get lascivious with* **Adela**. **Father** *watches from the table.*

Father   Do you understand the horrible cynicism of this symbol on a woman's foot, Joseph? Of her licentious walk on such elaborate heels, you do not understand. It's God's fault, God's to blame . . . For too long we have lived under the terror of the matchless perfection of the Creator. We don't wish to compete with him. We have no ambition to emulate him. We wish to be creators in our own lower sphere; we want to have the privilege of creation, we want creative delights, we want, in one word, godliness.

> My father, exhausted by the heat . . . shook himself violently, buzzed, and rose in fright before our eyes, transformed into a monstrous, hairy steel blue horsefly . . . we recognised that my father's transformation was a symbol of an inner protest, a violent and desperate demonstration of suffering. *The Dead Season*

Father, *infuriated, leaps down from the table.*

The sound of flies buzzing

Everyone tries to swat the swarm of flies which has descended on them. **Adela** *DSL holding the fly swat, grabs one fly.*

Buzzing stops.

Silence. Everyone stops for a moment of complete immobility. She releases the fly.

The buzzing re-starts.

Father *begins to turn into a fly. He buzzes round the* **Assistants** *and* **Adela**, *then* **Charles** *and* **Agatha** *and* **Emil**. *The* **Assistants** *take the ends of the tablecloth and it is caught up round* **Father***'s waist. He comes to DSC where he stands transfixed and buzzing furiously.* **Maria**, *unseen, makes his insect antennae with two forks above his head.* **Father** *releases himself from the cloth.* **Joseph** *follows the cloth as it is draped back over the table.* **Adela** *pursues a fly round the table in front of the diners, who push their chairs back to give her room. She kills the fly with her fly swatter.* **Father** *collapses DSC.*

8 The killing of the birds

> One day, during spring cleaning, Adela suddenly appeared in
> Father's bird kingdom . . . A fiendish cloud of feathers and wings
> arose screaming, and Adela, like a furious maenad protected by
> the whirlwind of her thyrsus, danced the dance of destruction . . .
> A moment later, my father came downstairs – a broken man, an
> exiled king who had lost his throne and his kingdom. *Birds*

Mother   Really, Jacob, having fallen into this lamentable
condition why have you not the strength of spirit or dignity
to bear it without complaint?

Leon *and* **Theodore** *pick up* **Father** *from the floor and replace
him on his chair.* **Adela** *takes the fly and drops it in the stove. All give
one last death-throe buzz.*

Father   Matter! (*He goes to the stove.*) We should weep when
we see the misery of that violated matter. (*He goes to the table,
clutching a pile of plates.*) Matter never makes jokes. Even this
plate has infinite fertility. In the depths of this clay indistinct
smiles are shaped, attempts at form appear . . .

Adela *takes the plate away from him.*

Father (*picks up a book*)   Do you understand the mystery of
these sheaves, these arabesques of Indian ink? . . .

Adela *takes the book from him. Birdshit falls on* **Charles** *twice.*
Emil *laughs and shit falls on him. As he complains, mouth open,
looking up, shit falls in his mouth. Soon it is raining birdshit.* **Father**
and **Joseph** *stand SR, watching. The others find umbrellas and try
to protect themselves, appalled.*

Adela (*grabs* **Father***'s egg*)   Enough is enough! (*She takes the
egg from* **Father** *and breaks it into a plate.*) I have had it up to
here! (*She storms DSL to the tap.*)

Father (*mournfully holding up the running egg yolk*)   I knew a
certain sea-captain who had in his cabin a lamp made by
Malayan embalmers from the body of his murdered
mistress.

In the stunned silence, **Mother** *speechlessly gropes for comfort, reason and laments her lot. Finally, she points in the direction of the attic and . . .*

Mother   These birds, these eggs Jacob, they're dreams, worthless dreams. Adela!

Adela   Frau Jacob.

Mother   They're in the attic!

Everyone points in the direction of the attic. **Adela** *strides towards her appointed task – to clear the attic of the birds.* **Adela** *climbs the ladder SR.*

Joseph   Mother, what are you doing?

While **Joseph** *is arguing with his family,* **Father** *attempts to follow* **Adela**. *He is held back by the* **Assistants**. *The stage darkens. The family become the birds in the attic.* **Father** *and* **Adela** *re-emerge USR, as if they have climbed to the top of the house.* **Joseph** *watches from DSR in horror.* **Adela** *and* **Father** *approach the table and hide behind it.* **Adela** *opens a desk lid. Light pours out. She is in the attic. She confronts the birds. The birds flap and squawk. Three times she tries to get rid of them. When they run from their position at the table USL, they trace a huge circle round the table to DSL.* **Adela** *picks up a broom and chases the birds until they gather DSL.*

Adela (*USR*)   Out!

She charges them and they fly in terror. **Father** *becomes a condor on the desks. The umbrellas become his flapping wings behind him.* **Adela** *charges the condor and kills it with her broom.*

9 Tango

> Lifting up with ease Adela's slim shoe, he spoke as if seduced by the lustrous eloquence of that empty shell of patent leather. 'Do you understand the horrible cynicism of this symbol on a woman's foot, the provocation of her licentious walk on such elaborate heels?' . . . *The Age of Genius*

Joseph   Adela . . .

The bird collapses.

Joseph   Adela . . .

The table disintegrates. **Joseph** *runs through it as the desks reassemble into the classroom. He is prevented from reaching* **Adela** *by the swinging desks. The class re-emerges, seated at their desks.* **Adela** *sweeps* **Father**/*the dying condor wrapped in the cloth out through DSR doors.* **Father** *crawls like a cockroach.*

Adela (*sings*)
   All the birdies they are here
   All the birdies so dear
   Blackbird, thrush, finch and crow
   Sitting pretty in a row
   All the birdies they are set free
   Joyful blessed and happy

She returns to her desk.

Joseph (*goes to her angrily*)   Adela! (*He seizes her arm as if he will hit her.*)

Joseph   Adela . . . Adela!

She takes a glass and a spoon from her desk and gives them to him.

Adela   Joseph . . .

From out of his top pocket, she takes a letter. He tries to seize it back. She runs across the room, returning only the envelope. She reads.

'Dear Sir,
I need a friend. I need the closeness of a kindred spirit. I long for some outside affirmation of the inner world whose existence I cherish. I need a partner for voyages of discovery. One person becomes reality when reflected in two pairs of eyes.

Emil *beats the rhythm of the tango with his pair of scissors.*

My world has been waiting for this twosome, as it were. What was once a closed tight place with no further prospects now begins to ripen into colours in the distance, burst open and reveal its depths.' (*She throws away the letter.*)

Joseph *is utterly bewitched by her. The rest of the cast have collected their musical instruments. They play the beat of the tango.* **Leon** *emerges with his violin. He is dressed in black. The tango begins.* **Joseph** *and* **Adela** *dance. He caresses her foot. He crawls behind her heel as she walks towards the tap. He kneels in front of her. She fills his glass from the tap. What emerges is milk. She holds him to her breast and feeds him the milk with a spoon. She joins the group playing the tango, all looking at him.* **Joseph** *turns to face them. The music stops.*

Joseph   Why are you doing this? Where is Father?

The band go crazy with a cacophonous din, laughing and playing.

No!

He throws the milk away. The figures around him fall to the ground, taking the rhythm of the wind in their bodies and still holding their instruments. Only **Leon** *continues to play the violin, like the figure of Death.* **Joseph** *rushes past him looking up at the back wall where* **Father** *sat in the shop.*

Father, Father.

Leon *plays a final note on his violin. The tap begins to run of its own accord. Everyone looks at it.* **Adela** *goes to turn it off. As she gets back to her desk,* **Joseph** *seizes her by the arm.*

Adela, where is Father? Adela, please, tell me where is Father?

Agatha *hands* **Joseph** *a book.*

Charles   Page twenty-two.

All

> Wer reitet so spät durch Nacht und Wind?
> Es ist der Vater . . .

Joseph   . . . Father.

All

... mit seinem Kind.
Er hat den Knaben wohl in dem Arm

Joseph   Mother, Mother, where are you going? Where is Father?

Joseph *runs USC to where* **Mother** *sits. She is putting on her hat and coat and gloves.*

Mother   Joseph, I had to get rid of them. They were very noisy and dirty.

All

Wer reitet so spät durch Nacht und Wind?
Es ist der Vater ...

Joseph   Where is Father? Mother, I'm asking you. What have you done with Father?

Part Three: The Republic of Dreams

1 The branch line of time

> The train, which ran only once a week on that forgotten branch line, carried no more than a few passengers. Never before had I seen such archaic coaches . . . they exuded an air of strange and frightening neglect . . . Conductor where are you? *Sanatorium under the Sign of the Hourglass*

Joseph *bangs the lid of* **Mother***'s desk in fury. Again, as in a nightmare – as if propelled by the violence of his action – the class hurl themselves at the floor as if thrown by an invisible hand.*

All

Wer reitet so spät . . .

Wer reitet so spät . . .

Wer reitet so spät . . .

The class rise and fall with the words, gradually crawling DSC. Confused, **Joseph** *comes between them, trying to lift them.* **Theodore** *gives him a suitcase. The class reassemble DSC as a train, sitting on their chairs which they have brought with them. Their words form the rhythm of the train moving. This rhythm continues underneath the whole of the next scene.*

All

Wer reitet so spät . . .

Wer reitet so spät . . .

Wer reitet so spät . . .

The group move as if on a rattling 1930s train. **Joseph** *clutches his suitcase. For some reason, he is wearing* **Charles***' hat.* **Charles** *irritably takes it back. They are now sitting in this order:*

| Maria | Theodore | | Charles | Agatha |
| Mother | Adela | | Emil | Joseph |

Joseph   Mother! Mother!

Leon, *still dressed in black as the figure of Death, appears upstage of them as the ticket collector.*

Leon   Billets!!

Joseph   Mother. Where are we going, Mother?

Mother   Be quiet, Joseph, we're nearly there.

Leon   Bitte! Billets!!

Emil (*pointing to* **Joseph**'s *suitcase*)   Luggage! Luggage!

Joseph *tries to put his suitcase up on the rack. Everyone stands up to help. They form the wall of a corridor upstage of the chairs.*

Joseph   Mother! Mother!

Charles   Don't push!

The scream of train brakes.

The group hurtle upstage into the darkness. **Joseph**'s *suitcase is flung back at him as the train stops.*

2 The sanatorium

In the hallway of the many windowed hotel that advertised itself
as the Sanatorium, there was semi-darkness and a solemn silence.
Dr Gotard was standing in the middle of the room to receive me.
'None of our patients know or can guess that the whole secret of
the operation is that we have put back the clock. Here your
father's death, the death that has already struck him in your
country, has not occurred yet . . .' *Sanatorium under the Sign of the
Hourglass*

Joseph *finds himself in somewhere completely new.* **Leon** *is
slumped over the DSR desk.* **Theodore** *sleeps on the USC desk.
Otherwise the room is empty.*

Joseph (*to* **Theodore**)   Excuse me.

Silence.

(*to* **Leon**)   Excuse me . . .

Leon   Maid!

Joseph   Excuse me . . . I am looking for my father.

Leon   Maid!

Agatha *appears from USL doors, dressed as a nurse. She rearranges the desks on SL to form a bed.*

Joseph   Excuse me.

Agatha   Ssshh!

Joseph   I am looking for my father.

Agatha (*lays out a sheet on the bed*)   Ssshh! Everyone is asleep now.

Joseph   Asleep? During the day?

Agatha   All the time. It's always night here. Perhaps you could wait in the restaurant. (*She crosses to go out of DSR doors.*) When the doctor wakes up, I'll let him know you're here. (*She exits, laughing DSR.*)

Joseph *follows her.* **Leon** *suddenly sits up, frightening* **Joseph**. **Leon** *is still dressed in black as the figure of Death.*

Leon   We received your telegram. Are you well?

Joseph Is my father still alive?

Leon   Of course. Within certain limits. In your country, your father is dead, but here he is very much alive. Here we turn back the clock. Go straight through. It's the first door. The first door!

Joseph *advances DSR.* **Leon** *exits USL.*

Father (*appears on the back wall*)   The six days of Creation were divine and bright. But on the seventh day, God broke down.

Joseph   Father!

Father   How good of you to come . . .

Enter everyone, except for **Mother**, *as a group. They gaze at* **Joseph**.

. . . but why did you bring so many? So many . . . so many . . . so many?

Maria *comes between* **Father** *and* **Joseph**. *Laughing, she pushes him DSR. The rest of the group rush* **Father** *to the bed DSL.*

Maria (*to* **Joseph**)   I think he'll recognize you.

Father   He felt an unknown texture beneath his fingers and, frightened, withdrew from the world. (*He gets into bed behind a sheet held by* **Adela** *and* **Agatha**.)

Maria *runs in front of the bed and presents* **Father**.

Maria   Well?

Maria, *singing a little nursery song, suddenly whips out her half a plate and reveals herself as the lover from the beginning of the play.* **Joseph** *is confused. As he looks for his half,* **Leon**, **Theodore** *and* **Maria** *laugh at him and disappear into the darkness.*

Joseph   Hey! Hey!

Adela   Joseph!

Joseph   Adela!

Adela   What are you doing out of bed?

Father   No, don't go, please don't go.

Joseph *is about to get into bed when he notices a light coming out of the DSR doors. They swing open.*

Mother   Ah, Joseph, there you are.

Joseph   Mother!

> My father was slowly failing, wilting before our eyes. Hunched among the enormous pillows, his grey hair standing wildly on end, he talked to himself in undertones. It seemed as if his personality had split into a number of opposing and quarrelling selves; he argued loudly with himself, persuading forcibly and passionately, pleading and begging. *Visitation*

Father (*to* **Adela**)   I see you've polished your shoes.

Joseph *gets into bed with* **Father** *who is continuing his discussion with himself.* **Adela** *gives* **Father** *a glass of medicine, which is apparently not to his liking.*

Father   No, no, no, there is no dead matter. Lifelessness is only a disguise . . . I can't account for the seasons. Oh, Jacob, Jacob, Jacob . . . What? Yes? Yes? (*To* **Joseph**.) A boy in a million, a ministering angel. You must agree, gentlemen, he is a charmer. We have lived too long under the natural perfection of the Creator. Is that a smoking jacket? There is nothing to be done about this plague of dogs for example. (*Pointing.*) Look! The anarchist Luccheni . . . (*Pointing in another direction.*) Draga . . . The hope and pride of his ancient family ruined by the unfortunate habit of masturbation. Well, we need the privilege of creation, we want creative delights, we want, in one word, godliness . . .

Joseph   Father –

Father   Godliness!! (*He disappears under the sheets.*)

Joseph   Mother, where am I? What's happening here?

Mother   Ah, Joseph, now don't be frightened – it's only the wind. (*She comforts* **Joseph**.)
　　Wer reitet so spät durch Nacht und Wind?
　　Es ist der Vater mit seinem Kind.
　　Er hat den Knaben wohl in dem Arm
　　Er fasst ihn sicher er halt ihn warm,

Father (*reappears from under the sheets*)   Look after the shop, Joseph. Look to the shop. Ah, what a relief it would be for the world to lose some of its contents . . . just some of its contents . . .

Mother
　　Mein Sohn, was birgst du so bang dein Gesicht
　　Siehst, Vater, du den Erlkönig nicht
　　Den Erlenkönig mit Kron und Schweif?
　　Mein Sohn, es ist ein Nebelstreif.

Joseph *suddenly whips back the sheet. Instead of* **Father**'s *head, there is now* **Charles**'. **Joseph** *leaps out of bed and stands before them all, confronting his* **Mother**.

O Vater, O Vater, und hörest du nicht
Was Erlenkönig mir leise verspricht?

Joseph   Mother –

Mother

Sei ruhig, bleibe ruhig, mein Kind
In durren Blättern sauselt der Wind.

She whips off the sheet revealing a pair of wooden dummy legs. **Emil** *puts them upright.*

There he is! He's a little thinner to be sure,

Theodore *and* **Leon** *appear above the legs with a set of dummy arms.* **Charles** *presents a dummy head of* **Father** *above this grotesquely assembled lifesize marionette which reminds us of* **Father**.

. . . but he's well on the way to recovery.

Emil   He's off his head!

Everybody laughs viciously. The group steps the dummy towards **Joseph**. *He runs round the class, the dummy pursuing him, until it dances in front of him DSC.*

Joseph   Stop it! (*He starts to wrestle with the dummy. It disintegrates in front of him. To* **Adela** *who has the legs.*) Get rid of it!

He watches in horror as **Adela** *is given a saw by* **Leon** *and she starts to saw the legs into small bits. As the legs are sawn, so* **Joseph**'s *legs seem to collapse themselves.*

Joseph   Oh Mother!

Mother

Ich liebe dich, mich reizt deine schone Gestalt
Und bist du nicht willig, so brauch ich Gewalt
O Vater, O Vater, jetzt fasst er mich an!
Erlkönig hat mir ein Leids getan!

Dem Vater grausets, er reitet geschwind,
Er halt in Armen das achzende Kind
Erreicht den Hof mit Mühe und Not
In seinem Armen das Kind war tot.

Adela *finishes sawing through the first leg. The wood falls to the floor.*

Joseph   Dead! Mother! Father is dead!

> My mother rushed in, frightened and enfolded my screams with
> her arms, wanting to stifle them like flames and choke them in the
> warmth of her love. She closed my mouth with hers and screamed
> together with me. *The Age of Genius*

Mother   Don't torture me. Your Father's away on a
business trip. He leaves very early in the morning and
comes back very late at night.

Joseph   Mother the shop! We must look after the shop!
(*He hurls* **Mother** *onto a desk.*) The shop!

*He violently creates the counter of the shop by straightening the desks
behind which the rest of the characters are sheltering. He appears to
pick up the entire line of desks by himself and they crash down in the
position of the original shop counter.*

3 The empty shop

> I had a hidden resentment against my mother for the ease with
> which she had recovered from Father's death. She had never
> loved him, I thought . . . *Cockroaches*

Joseph's *growing sense of desperation in this scene is not only about
an attempt to reverse time and refind his childhood but also a sense of
foreboding about the future. In the repetition of the gestures, he not only
expresses his anger and hurt at the disappearance of his father and by
extension his past, but also is attempting in some way to hold up time.*

Joseph (*bangs shut the desk lids*)   The shop! (*He forces*
Theodore *to ring the bell.*) Come in!

Charles   Good morning.

Emil   Good morning?

Agatha   Yes.

Joseph   Open the shop!

Assistants   Djin dobre.

Joseph dances with **Mother**. *The* **Assistants** *take off her coat. The taking off turns into a routine, which doesn't work.* **Mother** *stands on the counter. As in the first shop,* **Charles**, **Agatha** *and* **Emil** *appear as shoppers.*

Joseph   Open the shop.

The routine of coming into the shop with **Theodore** *ringing the bell,* **Leon** *opening the door with the door handle, the shoppers crossing from DSL to DSR, briefly watching* **Adela** *sawing* **Father**'s *legs [which she does continuously through this scene] and then stopping at DSL corner of the counter to ask* **Mother** *and the* **Assistants** *if they can buy something is a physical journey which is repeated almost exactly all three times. When the shoppers arrive in position,* **Mother** *raises her hand.*

Mother   And how can we help you?

Emil   Herr Jacob?

Mother   Herr Jacob?

Everyone momentarily looks at the remains of the marionette which **Adela** *is sawing up.*

Emil   I'd like a Royal tartan, please.

Assistants, *extremely rapidly, look in the desks. There is nothing there.*

Mother   I'm so sorry, we have nothing left.

The Assistants   Niet material!

Another block of wood drops from **Adela**'s *saw.*

Joseph   No . . . !

Maria *throws the ledger on the floor.*

Mother the shop! It is wrong! Do it again.

He throws the shoppers out, cruelly throws his **Mother** *out and makes them do the whole routine again. This time it is a little shorter. All the figures are a little more delapidated. No-one understands why they are being forced to do this.*

Joseph   Come in, come in . . .!

The bell rings. The shoppers enter. They end up in the same position at the DSL end of the counter.

Mother (*raises her hand*)   And how can we help you?

All momentarily glance once more at Father being chopped up.

Emil   I'd like a Persian cadar please.

Assistants, *extremely rapidly, look in the desks. There is nothing there.*

Mother   I'm so sorry, we have nothing left.

Assistants   Niet material!

Another block of wood drops from **Adela**'s *saw.*

Joseph   No!

Maria *throws the ledger on the floor.*

Joseph   Do it again! Again! Do it again!

Mother   Joseph.

Joseph   Mother!

Joseph   Come in, come in . . . ! (*He swings his* **Mother** *around and throws her against the counter.*)

The bell rings. The shoppers enter. They end up in the same position at the DSL end of the counter.

Mother (*raises her hand, sobbing*) And how can we help you?

All momentarily glance once more at **Father** *being chopped up.*

Emil   I'd like a Royal tartan, a Persian cadar, an electric bell –

Charles   The calaphony –

Emil   The calaphony from Malabar.

Assistants, *extremely rapidly, look in the desks. There is nothing there.*

Mother   I'm so very sorry, but we have absolutely nothing left.

Assistants   Niet material!

Joseph   No!

Joseph *swings* **Mother** *around. She begins to turn on the spot. Everybody is turning as at the end of a nightmare.* **Mother** *crashes to the floor. The sound of a door-slam. A final block of wood falls from* **Adela***'s saw. She picks up all the wood, puts it on her tray and goes USR to the stove. She loads the stove with wood. Takes out a match and lights it. She slams the top of the stove.*

4 The landau – Mother's story

The image of the landau was very important to Bruno. Throughout his childhood he drew this picture again and again . . . *Notes to the company from Jacob Schulz, Bruno's nephew, June 1992*

Seduced by my mother's caresses, I forgot my father, and my life began to run along a new and different track with no holidays and no miracles. *The Book*

Maria   Dinner's ready.

Joseph *tries to pick* **Mother** *up.* **Maria** *pushes him away.*

Charles (*reprovingly*)   Joseph.

Maria *takes* **Mother** *on her back and moves slowly to the dinner table. The shop counter now becomes the table.* **Adela** *and* **Leon** *cover it with a tablecloth.* **Joseph** *remains DSR looking out at the audience in defeat.* **Mother** *sits.*

Joseph Mother, I'm sorry Mother. I was trying to remember better times. (*He sits beside* **Mother**.) Times when we used to ride in our old landau.

Adela *and* **Maria** *USR of the table hand plates to* **Joseph** *who passes them to* **Mother**, **Agatha** *and* **Charles**. **Emil** *sits opposite SR of the table. Everyone is tired, dishevelled and forlorn.*

Mother Ah, yes! We used to ride in our old landau with its enormous hood. At dusk we came to the the last turning in the road. There was a rotting frontier post with a faded inscription on a board that was swaying in the wind. The wheels of the landau sank in the sand, the chattering spokes fell silent.

From SL, the assistants wheel in **Father** *on a trolley. He is immobile, in a black coat, like a waxwork. During the speech, very slowly, they bring him to the table, without* **Joseph** *noticing.*

We paid the toll, the turnpike squeaked and we drove on into a forest. The trees were dry and smelled like cigars, the thickets were dry fluff and the leaves were tobacco-coloured. As we drove on the forest became darker and darker and smelled more and more aromatically of tobacco, until at last it enclosed us entirely like a box of havanas. The coachman couldn't light the lanterns. He had no matches. And breathing very heavily, the horses found their way home by instinct as we rolled on and on into . . . autumn.

5 Autumn

Autumn is a huge touring show . . . it is a time of great confusion: everybody is pulling at the curtain ropes, and the sky, a great autumnal sky, hangs in tatters and is filled with the screeching of pulleys . . . there is an atmosphere of feverish haste, of belated carnival, a ballroom about to empty in the small hours, a panic of masked people who cannot find their real clothes. *A Second Fall*

Charles *takes off his hat out of which fall autumn leaves, lights a cigar and watches leaves fluttering down DSL.* **Maria** *and* **Adela** *part to reveal* **Father**.

Joseph (*turns to see his* **Father** *once more. He is delighted.*)
Father . . . Father (*Turns to* **Mother**.) Mother, Father is still
alive . . .

Mother   Of course he's still alive, he's at the dinner table.

Joseph   Father . . . How wonderful to see you. But why
are you wearing your coat at the table, Father?

There is no response from **Father**. **Joseph** *sits down, despondent.
Then he has an idea. He will try playing a joke he used to play with*
Father.

Joseph   Father . . . do you remember?

He turns **Charles***' cigar round the wrong way.* **Charles***' response
to sucking the hot coal is muted and automatic.*

Charles   Argh!

All look at **Joseph**.

Joseph (*goes to* **Father** *and clasps him by his hand*)   Father.
Oh, Father. (*It is a dummy hand and comes away in his own. He
throws it away in horror.*)

6 The Gale

> Night came. The wind intensified in force and violence. There, in
> those charred, many-raftered forests of attics, darkness began to
> degenerate and ferment wildly . . . *The Gale*

The desks begin to shift, as if by themselves. **Joseph** *throws himself
onto the desks, trying to gain control of the situation, as if his fantasy
had a life of its own.*

Pots and pans begin to rattle in the attic.

All look up.

Charles   I think there's a storm brewing.

Emil   Un tornado!

Mother   You won't be going to school today, Joseph, there's a gale blowing.

Agatha   Close the shutters or we'll lose our soup!

Leon *goes to close the DSR doors, which are rattling.*

Charles   You know, Joseph, I remember a wind so strong we had to put brass pestles and flat irons in our pockets . . .

The door flies open as **Leon** *reaches it. A blast of wind blows the tablecloth and all the people into a great sideways leaning picture.* **Father** *disappears SL. The door is slammed shut. Everyone is slumped over the table.* **Father** *has disappeared.*

Joseph   Father!

The hand that fell out of **Father***'s arm rears up mysteriously and takes possession of the cloth, with* **Emil** *and* **Charles** *holding on to either side of it, it propels* **Joseph** *DSC where he seems to fight with this wooden hand. They move to the door to attempt to throw it away. The door bursts open once more. Another creature is caught in the sheet. A form pressing against it, like a furey. The sheet whips away, revealing a girl dressed in black. It is* **Maria** *with half a plate. The rest of the cast are blown by this blast to the USL corner.* **Joseph** *frantically tries to get to* **Maria***. She is sucked once more out of the door. The rest of the cast are sucked back to their individual desks, which have come apart from the table. They slump over the desks. They are a grotesque repetition of the happy children in the first class. They look like Death. As* **Joseph** *goes to each desk in turn, it opens. Light pours out of it. They begin once more to repeat – mantra-like – 'Der Erlkönig'.*

Class
　Wer reitet so spät durch Nacht und Wind? . . .

Maria, *as the embodiment of the gale bursts in USL and threatens everyone as she comes DSL. The group staggers USR opposite* **Maria***. The gale/* **Maria** *mocks* **Joseph** *and produces a half-broken plate.* **Joseph** *finds the other half in his pocket and approaches her with it in desperation. The group hold* **Joseph** *by his coat tails and flap as they cross diagonally to* **Maria***.* **Maria** *removes her*

coat. She is naked beneath it. She is the ideal of the woman that
Joseph *dreams about and constantly draws.* **Joseph** *almost reaches*
her, their broken halves almost meet, but the gale capriciously whisks
her half away at the last moment. **Joseph** *falls. The group whirls*
away and disappears DSR. **Joseph** *chases* **Maria** *through the*
desks and out DSR. As he shuts the door he still has a flapping shawl
in his hands. He thrusts it into the stove. A jet of flame bursts from the
stove.

The sound of marching feet.

Joseph *returns to set desks in line facing the US wall. He is trying to*
reconstitute the shop as it was.

Part Four: The Act of Destruction

1 The worshippers of Baal

The time of the Great Season was approaching. The streets were getting busy. At six in the evening the city became feverish, the houses stood flushed, and people walked about made up in bright colours, illuminated by some interior fire, their eyes shining with a festive fever, beautiful yet evil. *The Night of the Great Season*

Joseph *alone behind the desks.*

The sound of marching feet dies away.

Joseph (*desperately tries the bell. It no longer rings.*)　Kling! Kling!

Doors fly open USL. Enter the shoppers. They are keen to buy. They walk describing an ominous square space around the shop.

Joseph　Hey! Hey! The shop is closed!

The shoppers continue to walk. **Joseph** *is confused. On the final side of the square, advancing from USC to DSL, the shoppers suddenly turn and point at* **Joseph**'s *shop as if this is the one they want. They then peel round, one behind the other until they are in the USL corner, pointing at things in the shop, talking excitely, imploring* **Joseph** *to open the shop and start selling to them. They come to the door. They knock on the windows looking at all the things that they want to buy.*

Theodore　Come on Joseph, open up, we've been here long enough.

Joseph　The shop is closed. Come back tomorrow!

Emil　Abri la tienda a hora!

Mother　Absolutely!

Joseph　I'm sorry but we are in the middle of stocktaking.

Leon　Auf die Tür! Heute schwimmen wir im Geld!

Everybody laughs.

Their chorus of demands to **Joseph** *to open the shop grow and grow until they break into song: 'Worthy is the Lamb' from Handel's* Messiah, *led by* **Charles**.

Charles   Joseph, Joseph, open the shop.

All (*laugh*)
   Joseph, Joseph, open the shop.
   For you must trade with us and sell us your cloth
   To receive power and riches and wisdom and strength
   And honour and glory and blessing.

(*much quieter*)
   Joseph, Joseph, open the shop.

Joseph   Go away.

All
   For you must trade with us and sell us your cloth
   To receive power and riches and wisdom and strength
   And honour and glory and blessing.

The group breaks once more into the cacophony of demands. **Leon** *finds the door handle, places it and orchestrates the group to all push together. They break into the shop. Slow motion.* **Theodore** *produces the bell and rings it. Bell and handles go into the stove. The group turns.*

All (*very delicate singing as they move forward to the position behind the desks*)
   Worthy is the Lamb that was slain
   And hath redeemed us to God by his blood
   To receive power and riches and wisdom and strength
   And honour and glory and blessing.

They advance towards the counter. They start to open the desks and look at what is inside. **Joseph** *tries to stop them and then gives up. In despair,* **Joseph** *takes his chair and sits.*
   Worthy is the Lamb that was slain
   And hath redeemed us to God by his blood
   To receive power and riches and wisdom and strength
   And honour and glory and blessing.

Theodore *and* **Leon** *slam DSR desktops shut. All straighten up.*

Mother   Well of course I saw them only very recently and you know what people say.

Agatha   A rolling stone gathers no moss.

Emil   Un artista! That's what he thinks he is.

Theodore   Which is exactly what I said last week.

A rhythmic cacophony of agreement and observation.

Charles (*sees what he is after*)   Well, look at that for a piece of cloth!

The shoppers burst through the counter. **Adela** *and* **Theodore** *throw themselves onto a big blue cloth DSL. They stretch it out in front of* **Joseph***, who is surrounded by the other shoppers. They hold it up to him.* **Emil** *pulls a beautiful piece of cloth out of the flies SL whilst SR* **Charles** *unrolls the cloth that* **Father** *had put up in the first scene of the show. They cross each other, grabbing and tearing at them in their impatience.* **Father, Theodore, Charles, Emil, Leon** *raise* **Joseph***'s chair and take him to the back wall where they place him on a chairlift, which winches him up overlooking the entire stage and the action, high up and powerless to intervene. Other white silks fall from the ceiling. They see high above USL a shelf containing cloth.*

Theodore   That's the one I want.

The shoppers build a tower of desks in order to try and reach this cloth USL. **Theodore** *climbs. His chair 'falls' to simulate a fake accident. It is caught by* **Charles** *or* **Emil** *who crashes to the ground in a mock fall.* **Theodore** *climbs onto pegs and then reaches the cloth. Shouted instructions between* **Mother, Joseph** *and* **Theodore***. The landscape cloth tumbles. It covers the entire stage. The group stretch it out. It is supported by two poles, goes over the desks and is part attached to the original shelf where* **Theodore** *pulled it from and held in the lap of* **Joseph** *sitting halfway up the wall. It forms a huge landscape-like expanse onto which are projected moving cloud bursts.*

Joseph   'And when Moses saw this, his anger burned
within him. And he threw the tables of the Commandments
and he broke them at the foot of the Mountain. And he took
the calf that they had made and burned it in the fire, ground
it into powder and made the children of Israel drink it. And
turning to Aaron he said, "What did these people unto thee,
that thou hast brought so great a sin upon them?" And
Aaron said "Let not the anger of my Lord wax hot. Thou
knowest the people that they are set on mischief."'

*From beneath the landscape, the group emerges holding books and
ledgers above their heads like birds. They cross to DSR.* **Joseph** *sees
them and recognizes some of the birds.*

2 The fall of birds

And soon the sky came out in a coloured rash, in blotches which
grew and spread, and was filled with a strange tribe of birds. They
were the distant, forgotten progeny of that generation of birds
which at one time Adela had chased away to all four points of the
sky. All of a sudden stones began to whistle through the air. The
stupid, thoughtless people had begun to throw them into the
fantastic bird-filled sky. *The Night of the Great Season*

Joseph   Father, the birds have come back, Father. Look!
The condor and the wrens from England.

When they reach DSR the birds become people again. **Theodore**
appears as a bird at the top of ladder stage left. **Emil** *throws a book
directly at him.* **Theodore** *(as the bird) flaps and falls to the floor.*
Emil *drags him centre stage in the middle of the white cloth. The
black coats/the shoppers surround him and begin to stone him with
books. He struggles and writhes on the sheet. The crowd fold up the
cloth. It becomes very dark. The cloth is pulled very slowly in a
procession DSR.* **Leon** *opens a trap door in the floor. Light pours out.
There is no other light. Everybody and everything in the cloth gradually
slides into the trap and disappears extremely slowly.* **Joseph** *has come
off his seat on the back wall. He is clasping his chair to his chest. As
the trap door closes, he sits on his chair DSC. He lifts his book. He is*

in the position that he was at the very beginning of the show. He looks out into the audience.

Once more, the sound of marching feet.

Epilogue

19 November 1942

On a day I don't recall in 1942, known as Black Thursday in
Drohobycz, the Gestapo carried out a massacre in the ghetto. We
happened to be in the ghetto to buy food [instead of at work
outside]. When we heard shooting and saw Jews run for their lives
we too took to flight. Schulz, physically the weaker, was caught by
a Gestapo agent called Guenther, who stopped him, put a
revolver to his head, and fired twice. *Letter to Jerzy Ficowski from
Tadeusz Lubowiecki, Gilwice, 1949.*

Upstage, across from one side to the other are nine chairs. **Joseph***'s
characters run from USL to USR and stop, each one standing beside a
chair. They are in this order:*

Adela Theodore Maria Leon Agatha Charles Emil Mother Father

The sound of marching feet fades away.

*The characters behind their chairs turn, look out into the audience and
sit down.* **Theodore** *begins to march whilst seated. The rest of the
characters join in with him. It is the same rhythm that we have heard
from marching feet all the way through the show.* **Joseph** *hears the
sound of marching feet and is frightened. He backs off upstage, running
to and fro as if he can now really see soldiers coming and closing in on
him; as if he is surrounded by a reality we cannot see. He finds himself
between the seated* **Leon** *and* **Agatha***.* **Leon** *holds him by the arm.*

Theodore   Company halt!

The characters stop marching. **Agatha** *stands on her chair and makes
the sign of a gun against his temple. The sound of a real gunshot, loud.*
Joseph *staggers forward. His book drops beside him. He totters to
his chair. He takes off his jacket and drops it. Then his tie. He removes
his shoes. He returns to the end of the line upstage where he removes his
shirt and trousers. He falls into his* **Father***'s arms wearing only socks
and underpants. His* **Father** *cradles him like a baby and passes him
in this infant position to* **Mother***, next to him, where now we see that
he looks like a pieta. He is passed all the way along the line of actors.*
Adela*, the last, stands with him in her arms. She walks directly SL*

and the rest of the cast stand up. She turns downstage. The group gather round her. They gently walk a few steps towards the audience. They stop. With **Joseph** *in her arms, for a moment, they look at the audience.* **Adela** *starts to walk backwards and gradually they all turn away and exit through the USL double doors.*

Disappearing into the light.

A SELECTED LIST OF
METHUEN MODERN PLAYS

☐ CLOSER	Patrick Marber	£6.99
☐ THE BEAUTY QUEEN OF LEENANE	Martin McDonagh	£6.99
☐ A SKULL IN CONNEMARA	Martin McDonagh	£6.99
☐ THE LONESOME WEST	Martin McDonagh	£6.99
☐ THE CRIPPLE OF INISHMAAN	Martin McDonagh	£6.99
☐ THE STEWARD OF CHRISTENDOM	Sebastian Barry	£6.99
☐ SHOPPING AND F***ING	Mark Ravenhill	£6.99
☐ FAUST (FAUST IS DEAD)	Mark Ravenhill	£5.99
☐ POLYGRAPH	Robert Lepage and Marie Brassard	£6.99
☐ BEAUTIFUL THING	Jonathan Harvey	£6.99
☐ MEMORY OF WATER & FIVE KINDS OF SILENCE	Shelagh Stephenson	£7.99
☐ WISHBONES	Lucinda Coxon	£6.99
☐ BONDAGERS & THE STRAW CHAIR	Sue Glover	£9.99
☐ SOME VOICES & PALE HORSE	Joe Penhall	£7.99
☐ KNIVES IN HENS	David Harrower	£6.99
☐ BOYS' LIFE & SEARCH AND DESTROY	Howard Korder	£8.99
☐ THE LIGHTS	Howard Korder	£6.99
☐ SERVING IT UP & A WEEK WITH TONY	David Eldridge	£8.99
☐ INSIDE TRADING	Malcolm Bradbury	£6.99
☐ MASTERCLASS	Terrence McNally	£5.99
☐ EUROPE & THE ARCHITECT	David Grieg	£7.99
☐ BLUE MURDER	Peter Nichols	£6.99
☐ BLASTED & PHAEDRA'S LOVE	Sarah Kane	£7.99

METHUEN STUDENT EDITIONS

☐ SERJEANT MUSGRAVE'S DANCE	John Arden	£6.99
☐ CONFUSIONS	Alan Ayckbourn	£5.99
☐ THE ROVER	Aphra Behn	£5.99
☐ LEAR	Edward Bond	£6.99
☐ THE CAUCASIAN CHALK CIRCLE	Bertolt Brecht	£6.99
☐ MOTHER COURAGE AND HER CHILDREN	Bertolt Brecht	£6.99
☐ THE CHERRY ORCHARD	Anton Chekhov	£5.99
☐ TOP GIRLS	Caryl Churchill	£6.99
☐ A TASTE OF HONEY	Shelagh Delaney	£6.99
☐ STRIFE	John Galsworthy	£5.99
☐ ACROSS OKA	Robert Holman	£5.99
☐ A DOLL'S HOUSE	Henrik Ibsen	£5.99
☐ MY MOTHER SAID I NEVER SHOULD	Charlotte Keatley	£6.99
☐ DREAMS OF ANNE FRANK	Bernard Kops	£5.99
☐ BLOOD WEDDING	Federico Lorca	£5.99
☐ THE MALCONTENT	John Marston	£5.99
☐ BLOOD BROTHERS	Willy Russell	£6.99
☐ DEATH AND THE KING'S HORSEMAN	Wole Soyinka	£6.99
☐ THE PLAYBOY OF THE WESTERN WORLD	J.M. Synge	£5.99
☐ OUR COUNTRY'S GOOD	Timberlake Wertenbaker	£6.99
☐ THE IMPORTANCE OF BEING EARNEST	Oscar Wilde	£5.99
☐ A STREETCAR NAMED DESIRE	Tennessee Williams	£5.99

● All Methuen Drama books are available through mail order or from your local bookshop.

Please send cheque/eurocheque/postal order (sterling only) Access, Visa, Mastercard, Diners Card, Switch or Amex.

☐☐☐☐☐☐☐☐☐☐☐☐☐☐☐☐☐☐

Expiry Date: _____ Signature: _____

Please allow 75 pence per book for post and packing U.K.
Overseas customers please allow £1.00 per copy for post and packing.

ALL ORDERS TO:

Methuen Books, Books by Post, TBS Limited, The Book Service, Colchester Road, Frating Green, Colchester, Essex CO7 7DW.

NAME: _____

ADDRESS: _____

_____

Please allow 28 days for delivery. Please tick box if you do not wish to receive any additional information ☐

Prices and availability subject to change without notice.

METHUEN SCREENPLAYS

☐ BEAUTIFUL THING	Jonathan Harvey	£6.99
☐ THE ENGLISH PATIENT	Anthony Minghella	£7.99
☐ THE CRUCIBLE	Arthur Miller	£6.99
☐ THE WIND IN THE WILLOWS	Terry Jones	£7.99
☐ PERSUASION	Jane Austen, adapted by Nick Dear	£6.99
☐ TWELFTH NIGHT	Shakespeare, adapted by Trevor Nunn	£7.99
☐ THE KRAYS	Philip Ridley	£7.99
☐ THE AMERICAN DREAMS (THE REFLECTING SKIN & THE PASSION OF DARKLY NOON)	Philip Ridley	£8.99
☐ MRS BROWN	Jeremy Brock	£7.99
☐ THE GAMBLER	Dostoyevsky, adapted by Nick Dear	£7.99
☐ TROJAN EDDIE	Billy Roche	£7.99
☐ THE WINGS OF THE DOVE	Hossein Amini	£7.99
☐ THE ACID HOUSE TRILOGY	Irvine Welsh	£8.99
☐ THE LONG GOOD FRIDAY	Barrie Keeffe	£6.99
☐ SLING BLADE	Billy Bob Thornton	£7.99

• All Methuen Drama books are available through mail order or from your local bookshop.

Please send cheque/eurocheque/postal order (sterling only) Access, Visa, Mastercard, Diners Card, Switch or Amex.

☐☐☐☐☐☐☐☐☐☐☐☐☐☐☐☐

Expiry Date: _____ Signature: _____

Please allow 75 pence per book for post and packing U.K.
Overseas customers please allow £1.00 per copy for post and packing.

ALL ORDERS TO:

Methuen Books, Books by Post, TBS Limited, The Book Service, Colchester Road, Frating Green, Colchester, Essex CO7 7DW.

NAME: _____

ADDRESS: _____

_____

_____

Please allow 28 days for delivery. Please tick box if you do not wish to receive any additional information ☐

Prices and availability subject to change without notice.

METHUEN DRAMA
MONOLOGUE & SCENE BOOKS

☐ CONTEMPORARY SCENES FOR ACTORS (MEN)	Earley and Keil	£8.99
☐ CONTEMPORARY SCENES FOR ACTORS (WOMEN)	Earley and Keil	£8.99
☐ THE CLASSICAL MONOLOGUE (MEN)	Earley and Keil	£7.99
☐ THE CLASSICAL MONOLOGUE (WOMEN)	Earley and Keil	£7.99
☐ THE CONTEMPORARY MONOLOGUE (MEN)	Earley and Keil	£7.99
☐ THE CONTEMPORARY MONOLOGUE (WOMEN)	Earley and Keil	£7.99
☐ THE MODERN MONOLOGUE (MEN)	Earley and Keil	£7.99
☐ THE MODERN MONOLOGUE (WOMEN)	Earley and Keil	£7.99
☐ THE METHUEN AUDITION BOOK FOR MEN	Annika Bluhm	£6.99
☐ THE METHUEN AUDITION BOOK FOR WOMEN	Annika Bluhm	£6.99
☐ THE METHUEN AUDITION BOOK FOR YOUNG ACTORS	Anne Harvey	£6.99
☐ THE METHUEN BOOK OF DUOLOGUES FOR YOUNG ACTORS	Anne Harvey	£6.99

• All Methuen Drama books are available through mail order or from your local bookshop.

Please send cheque/eurocheque/postal order (sterling only) Access, Visa, Mastercard, Diners Card, Switch or Amex.

☐☐☐☐☐☐☐☐☐☐☐☐☐☐☐☐

Expiry Date:_____Signature:_____

Please allow 75 pence per book for post and packing U.K.
Overseas customers please allow £1.00 per copy for post and packing.

ALL ORDERS TO:

Methuen Books, Books by Post, TBS Limited, The Book Service, Colchester Road, Frating Green, Colchester, Essex CO7 7DW.

NAME:_____

ADDRESS:_____

_____

Please allow 28 days for delivery. Please tick box if you do not
wish to receive any additional information   ☐

Prices and availability subject to change without notice.

METHUEN CLASSICAL GREEK DRAMATISTS

☐ AESCHYLUS PLAYS: I (*Persians, Prometheus Bound, Suppliants, Seven Against Thebes*)   £9.99
☐ AESCHYLUS PLAYS: II (*Oresteia: Agamemnon, Libation-Bearers, Eumenides*)   £9.99
☐ SOPHOCLES PLAYS: I (*Oedipus the King, Oedipus at Colonus, Antigone*)   £9.99
☐ SOPHOCLES PLAYS: II (*Ajax, Women of Trachis, Electra, Philoctetes*)   £9.99
☐ EURIPIDES PLAYS: I (*Medea, The Phoenician Women, Bacchae*)   £9.99
☐ EURIPIDES PLAYS: II (*Hecuba, The Women of Troy, Iphigenia at Aulis, Cyclops*)   £9.99
☐ EURIPIDES PLAYS: III (*Alkestis, Helen, Ion*)   £9.99
☐ EURIPIDES PLAYS: IV (*Elektra, Orestes, Iphigeneia in Tauris*)   £9.99
☐ EURIPIDES PLAYS: V (*Andromache, Herakles' Children, Herakles*)   £9.99
☐ EURIPIDES PLAYS: VI (*Hippolytos Suppliants, Rhesos*)   £9.99
☐ ARISTOPHANES PLAYS: I (*Acharnians, Knights, Peace, Lysistrata*)   £9.99
☐ ARISTOPHANES PLAYS: II (*Wasps, Clouds, Birds, Festival Time, Frogs*)   £9.99
☐ ARISTOPHANES & MENANDER: NEW COMEDY (Aristophanes: *Women in Power, Wealth* Menander: *The Malcontent, The Woman from Samos*)   £9.99
